Little Miami Conservancy
Wild & Scenic River Conservation Since 1967

Steve Coomer's
Little Miami River

Fishing, Facts & Folklore Galore !

FIRST EDITION

Published under agreement with the
Little Miami Conservancy, 6040 Price Road, Milford OH 45150

PRINTED IN CANADA

ISBN 978-0-99604438-0-9

Disclaimer

DEDICATION
AND ACKNOWLEDGEMENTS

I'd like to dedicate this book to my father, the finest man I've ever known. What literary types might call a simple working man, he is anything but simple. He has always been filled with a deep and lifelong curiosity about the outdoors. To this day it's impossible to walk into his house and not be drawn into a conversation on the medicinal properties of goldenseal or the diet of piliated woodpeckers or any of a hundred other topics on the natural world.

I'd also like to thank *Vic Coomer* who was probably the only person who believed a good ole boy who fished every day could actually write a book about this wonderful river where I became me. I'd like to thank Bill Schroeder for organizing my mess of a first draft into book form, a herculean task I'm sure.

My biggest hope for this book is that it inspires a few people to get out there. To experience for themselves the wonderful streams and rivers we have right outside of town, right outside our own back doors. I remember the story of Swiss naturalist Jean Louis Agassiz who said "I spent the summer traveling; I got halfway across my back yard." Nature and beauty are not just at far away places seen only on the Discovery Channel, they are right here, all around us. Good fishing,

STEVE COOMER.

Steve Coomer's
Little Miami River

Table of Contents

APPENDIX

FOREWORD

By Bill Schroeder, Little Miami Conservancy Trustee and Buckeye United Fly Fishers Little Miami River Coordinator

In my wildest dreams, I never imagined there would ever be a comprehensive, informative book about Ohio's Little Miami River. In particular, I did not expect a book based on intimate knowledge, with insights into its ecology, marine life, fish, habitat, history, and culture, not to mention how to fish it all four seasons of the year.

Little did I know, such a work was well underway, already written, or nearly so. Who would write such a book, and why?

Enter Steven Coomer. Steve was born in South Lebanon, Ohio, one of the oldest communities along the banks of the Little Miami River. His dad was a hunter, fisherman, skilled taxidermist, and student of natural aspects of his environment. A business sign near his shop in South Lebanon used to say, "Coomer Taxidermy-Ginseng Root, bought and sold." His dad taught Steve skills and techniques for fishing and hunting along the Little Miami River. His mother, uncles, grandfather and brother also fished and shared a love of the outdoors. Most importantly, his upbringing as a youth kindled in Steve a passion for the Little Miami River (LMR) that remains a major influence in Steve's life today.

During 40-plus years fishing the LMR, Steve accumulated an enormous wealth of information and accomplished some remarkable things. He has analyzed the LMR fish, food chain and most of the market flies and lures to determine which ones work and why. He has devised unique techniques to get the right bait presented in the right place at the right time. He has designed and made his own flies and lures to mimic unique aquatic creatures in the LMR. He also worked out a plan to walk and fish the entire 105 miles of the river, studying structure, access points, riffles, old bridges, dams and other features that hold fish. So successful was Steve, that he began sharing what he learned, writing articles and producing a blog called Steven Outside, that has become quite successful. Along the way, the beginnings of a book emerged, ultimately leading to this work, **Steve Coomer's Little Miami River.**

In this book, Steve shares a wealth of "how to do" information about finding and catching fish on the LMR. Furthermore, the book is laced with anecdotal history, facts about environment, ecology, folklore, and legends about Tecumseh, Daniel Boone, Simon Kenton, and others, who knew and experienced the LMR over the past 250 years. Hence, it fulfills a promise to provide useful information, while also delivering fun reading, for all who are interested in the Little Miami River, and will hook those who may be just curious.   - Bill Schroeder

PART ONE

MY LITTLE MIAMI RIVER
Steve Coomer

I love the Little Miami River. Grew up on it. I'm guessing there are very few people who ever lived that have actually been lucky enough to fish it more. Like any great love there are heartaches. You lose a great fish. You get caught out in especially bad weather. You catch nothing but poison ivy. But the river has so much to give. Hang out along its banks long enough, and you can't help but have a fuller life because of it. Experience the quiet joy of a deer wading a riffle right after dawn, the thrill of a big smallmouth leaping, and the call of a barred owl while walking out at night. I don't give away any secret spots in this little book. I do mention some of the better-known places. Not that there aren't secret spots; there's plenty. But they are for you to discover on your own. I had a crazy idea once. So crazy I've never really told anyone about it. Years ago, I decided I was going to fish the length of the river or at least walk the length of it carrying a fishing rod looking for places to fish. Well over a decade later I haven't quite managed it, but I'm realizing it might just be possible after all. And let me tell you there are lots of secret spots. Old mill sites, broken dams, riffles out in the middle of nowhere, all waiting for someone to find them and make them their secret spot. Like any great love, you never stop discovering. Every time you're fishing, you catch little glimpses of the beauty you never realized was there. And the fishing is better than anyone knows.

Right now, as I'm writing this, it's nearing the end of the Fall fishing for smallmouth bass. The river is down to 54 degrees. In the last few weeks I've caught four 19-inch smallmouth and one 20-inch fish. And that's no fluke. There are bass like that up and down the length of the river. Hopefully this book can help you catch a few of them. There is also quite a bit on the LMR's big sister, the Great Miami River. The Great Miami also has some excellent fishing on it. There's one chapter in this book that is mostly about fishing the low head dams on the GMR for shovelheads. Just remember, you have to find your own way to transfer what you read to actual use on the water. Nothing beats time on the water. If you try, I can guarantee you will catch some fish. They are out there.

What's This Book About?

This book is not meant to be an exact (cast here, throw that) fishing guide to the Little Miami. Instead it's more the ramblings of a guy who has grown up around the river and seen most of it in a lifetime of fishing. There are individual sections on some of my favorite areas and a little background on each with a few fishing stories thrown in. Most people in the old photos are relatives of mine, or of places they worked or knew on the river. This is not a dry history from a textbook, but more along the lines of local lore and legend. And while I've tried to be accurate, don't take me as the gospel on these things.

After all, it is just possible that the Loveland Frog, the Hawnahooc or "River Demon" might not exist.

One nice thing about fishing the river is you don't need a twenty thousand dollar bass boat, and thousands more in equipment to have a quality experience. Steal your kid's book bag, throw inside a peanut butter sandwich, a water bottle, and a small box of lures, grab a fly rod or spinning rod, and you're all set. Put on some old tennis shoes that you won't mind getting wet. After all, that is probably the best way to experience the river, wading wet on a hot summer's day. As for lures, you don't need thousands. While the river's bass may be picky according to size or presentation, a dozen lures will cover just about every situation. The Little Miami is a river's river, and abounds with fish that will jump on a nightcrawler or live crayfish. A hellgrammite or small crayfish might just be the best option for smallmouth on the river too.

That's another nice thing about the river. Not only is it fine for classic fly fishing, where you can get as fancy as you want and spend more on a fly rod than you might on a decent used car, but the river is also ideal for just getting away, relaxing, and fishing the way Huck Finn might have, wading in old jeans and catching channel cats and drum on worms. A day on the Little Miami is a step back in time to the way fishing used to be, when the object was to get away and enjoy yourself. If you look around, you will also see things you had no idea existed in today's rushed world. Turtles digging nests in the sand, eagles flying overhead, a deer at the river at dusk. Try it, you just might like it.

What's This River About?

The Little Miami was one of the first streams named as part of the National Wild and Scenic Rivers System created by Congress in 1968, and the first in Ohio. To show just how rare an honor this is, nearby Kentucky has only one National Wild and Scenic River, while Indiana has none. Two other Ohio streams are recognized as National Wild and Scenic Rivers, Little Beaver Creek and Big & Little Darby. The Little Miami River flows over a hundred miles through Clermont, Clark, Montgomery, Greene, Warren, and Hamilton counties. This national designation, along with the Ohio Scenic River designation, were achieved by area conservation efforts spearheaded by Little Miami Inc. (LMI) in the '60s and '70s, to help assure that public projects will not adversely impact this national treasure. LMI's river conservation work continues today, under the organization's new name, Little Miami Conservancy (LMC), and citizens are encouraged to become members and support this important work.

The Little Miami River discharges somewhere around 1,700 cubic feet per second on average into the Ohio River each year. But during high water from heavy winter and spring rains, river flows may rise over 85,000 cubic feet per second. It continues to be rich in aquatic life that are all a part of the food chain, ideal habitat for a diverse population of fish.

Nowadays, you dip a minnow seine in the Little Miami, kick around a few rocks, and you have a net crawling with life. The Little Miami is home to somewhere around 90 species of fish. Several pollution intolerant species are among them, including slenderhead darters, northern madtoms, mountain madtoms, and black redhorse, that have expanded their numbers in the LMR since the 90's.

There are 38 species of mussels in the Little Miami, five of which are endangered. Did you know that collecting mussel shells from the river was once a thriving industry? And the Little Miami is still probably one of the best places in the world to find a freshwater pearl.

Oliver Watson wrote in the Dayton Sunday News in 1925, "Of all pearl producing streams in America, the Little Miami stands first in point of production, quality and value. One reason is that conditions are more favorable for the formation of a pearl for the pure condition of the water and the strong limestone deposits which add materially in the coating and polishing process through which the pearl passes." Israel Hopkins Harris owned the Little Miami Pearl Fisheries company in Waynesville and in 1888, he gathered over 2,000 pearls that were put on display at the Paris exposition. This collection of pearls was awarded a gold medal. Many items of jewelry made out of pearls and shells from the Little Miami have been excavated from Native American sites throughout the Midwest. The collection of pearls was also exhibited at the World's Fair at Chicago. The pearls were then sold to Tiffany & Company of New York. Something to think about when you're sitting on a sandbar in the Little Miami waiting for a channel cat to bite, and look down and see a pretty mussel shell. Of course, today collecting mussels from the river is no longer legal.

Over the years Michael A. Hoggarth, of the Department of Life and Earth Sciences at Otterbein College, has sampled mussel populations in the Little Miami and its tributaries, and is, best I can tell, the man when it comes to knowing what's up with mussels in the river. In a 2007 report on these populations he stated what I interpret as alarming conclusions, even though the water quality is improving greatly. His report states that populations of certain mussels are completely gone from the lower reaches of Todd's Fork, formerly listed as having good mussel faunas in 1990/91. This loss was attributed to excessive siltation. I know from personal experience, as you travel out of Morrow on Morrow-Woodville and Morrow-Blackhawk Roads, there are several fairly recent housing developments that have sprung up in just the last few years. And I see this pattern repeating itself all up and down Todd's Fork's watershed. It seems very important that natural forest buffer zones along rivers and streams be preserved. Fortunately, many developers have partnered with river conservation organizations, like the Little Miami Conservancy, to set aside such areas to protect and preserve wooded stream corridors, habitat and water quality. It is also essential that storm water and soil erosion controls be implemented and maintained at each development throughout the Little Miami's million-acre watershed.

Caesar Creek, at least from the dam down to the LMR, was also listed as having its native mussel populations decimated. Competition with introduced mollusks, the Asian clam and zebra mussel, appear to be culprits in losing the mussels in Caesar Creek. Zebra mussels are among the most prolific of all animals. An adult female zebra mussel may produce between 30,000 and a million eggs per year. Introducing these species could spell bad news long-term for the native species, and change the food chain in the river as a whole. I'm afraid this could be a case of the genie being out of the bottle, non-reversible. We may end up with more total mussels in the river in a few years, but less diversity, if the introduced species out-compete native mussels. Hoggarth's study found that lower reaches of the Little Miami have more diverse mussel faunas, but this is due to introducing species of mussels that use the freshwater drum as host. The freshwater drum, or sheephead, is expanding its range throughout the US. As anyone knows who's thrown a nightcrawler on a hook into the Little Miami in recent years, the freshwater drum is thriving in the river.

Some mussel populations in the middle reaches of the Little Miami River are holding their own, but others are doing less than that. Part of this is due to degradation of the riparian woodlands bordering the river. Keeping a buffer of woodland along the river and tributaries is key to insuring its health, a theme that cannot be overstated. Many species of mussels have been severely reduced in number over the years in the upper reaches of the Little Miami and tributaries, where there is less wooded land streamside to protect them from silt and chemicals applied as fertilizers. However, a remarkable turn-around of the Little Miami's fortunes has resulted from thousands of hours of hard work by volunteer stewardship organizations like the Little Miami Conservancy, and millions of dollars spent upgrading the watershed's waste treatment plants to meet the needs of growing population.

The Little Miami is almost two rivers in one. The upper river, from the headwaters above Clifton Gorge down to Waynesville, flows through what my copy of River and Stream Ecosystems of the World calls the central lowland province. The central lowland province is basically land that was bulldozed by the glaciers during the last ice age. This area, graded and shaped by the glaciers, is also known as the Till Plains. The lowlands are covered by a layer of glacial deposits that smooth the land's surface. These deposits also do something very important for the Little Miami River. They hold vast amounts of water underground and keep more water in the river during late summer and fall than most rivers of the same size. The Little Miami's lower half flows through gorges and deep valleys cut by the runoff of the same glaciers, melting as the last ice age ended. The river there has larger rocks in the riffles and a little less sand and gravel than the upper river. The lower river is much more heavily wooded than the upper river, different than most river systems. The lower river is right on the edge of the Interior Low Plateau, which is just a fancy name for the area south of the glacier's reach. This also is sometimes called the Drift Plain, in other scientific literature. The wooded hillsides of the lower Little Miami River valley and tributaries add lots of organic material in the form of fallen leaves and woody debris. In periods of high water, tons of broken down leaves and other organic matter are washed into the river adding to the diversity of the river's food chain. The Little Miami's mean annual load of this dissolved organic matter is over twice that of the Ohio River, into which the Little Miami flows. These same wooded margins of the river help protect it from agricultural silts and runoffs, which is also hugely important.

A 1991 study found an estimated 44% of the nitrogen and 28% of the phosphorus applied as fertilizer in the Mississippi River watershed entered its rivers and streams. Deposits of rocks, minerals, and silts washed into the rivers from elsewhere are called allochthonous inputs. No matter what they are called, these are bad news, smothering the tiny life that supports everything; another reason to protect the wooded lands remaining along the river. The importance of woodlands bordering the river was underscored by an Ohio EPA study of small tributaries running into the Little Miami River. This study found that the streams of the more heavily farmed Till Plains (upper river) had 1.7 times less riparian cover than those in the Drift Plain (lower river). This translated into about half as many larval forms of three taxa of aquatic insects: Empheroptera (mayflies), Plecoptera (stoneflies) and Tricoptera (caddisflies).

Protecting the lands bordering the river is key to protecting the river as well. Today, more than 50% of the Little Miami's riverbank forests are owned and protected by public agencies and private conservation groups like the Little Miami Conservancy. Such habitat preservation, along with reduced phosphorous loading from sewage treatment plants, as well as conservation plans on about 60% of the farms in the watershed, have been key to restoring the Little Miami River to "full attainment" of Ohio EPA's most stringent standards for biological and chemical levels. The Little Miami's ecosystem is among the top 10% of river ecosystems in Ohio.

Remarkably clean compared to nearby rivers, there remains one problem the Little Miami still has concerning water quality that is shared by most rivers and streams. That problem is the scourge of mercury. No matter how much is done to protect rivers from pollution from farming, industry, and waste treatment runoff, all of our streams are helpless against the buildup of mercury. Mercury enters the Little Miami's watershed every time it rains. Bacteria in the river ingest mercury from the rainwater that enters the tributaries and main stem. The mer-

cury then is passed to larger organisms that are eaten by even larger ones, and on and on, until the traces of mercury present in billions of tiny organisms are ultimately also in the river's larger fish, such as sauger and smallmouth bass. The Ohio Department of Natural Resources (DNR) recognizes the impact of mercury on the aquatic life in all rivers and streams, and fish consumption advisories are publicized for rivers and other public waters across the state, indicating which fish species are safe to consume, and in what quantities.

Even in the presence of tough stream water quality issues, such as the presence of mercury found in the food chain, several endangered fish species have been making a comeback in the Little Miami River. Two of these are the mountain madtom (a tiny catfish actually expanding its population in the Little Miami) and the blue sucker (entirely absent from the river for 40 years). The northern madtom is found only in a few places in Ohio, the Little Miami River being one. Another tiny fish, the slenderhead darter, has experienced a virtual population boom since the 1980's as the river has gotten cleaner. Furthermore, in 1998 the Ohio EPA collected a brindled madtom from the Little Miami, not collected since the 1950's. Other species considered threatened that have found refuge in the LMR include the bigeye shiner, tongue-tied minnow, and American eel. The American eel is an amazing animal called catadromous species, meaning it lives most of its life in freshwater, but spawns in saltwater. Some of these eels may have traveled over three thousand miles from the Gulf of Mexico, up the Mississippi River and the Ohio before finally reaching the Little Miami.

What fish in the Little Miami actually eat has always been of interest to me. Over time the Ohio DNR has built up a pretty good picture of this. Using their figures I have compiled this list:
Bottom-dwelling invertebrates (an animal without a backbone, insects, nymphs, worms) are eaten by 35% of the fish in the river, these include sculpins, madtoms, quite a few kinds of minnows, and most of the sucker and darter families. Invertebrates from all levels of a stream are eaten by 10% of the fishes, mudminnows, several true minnows, and many of the sunfishes like the longeared sunfish. Twenty per-

6

cent of the fish, (the real exciting ones) feed on fish and other aquatic vertebrates. These include crappies, smallmouth, largemouth and spotted bass, gar, musky, sunfish, saugeye, sauger, drum, and flathead catfish.

Fish that eat algae, plankton, plant debris, or are omnivores such as carp that eat everything takes up the rest of the totals. This group includes the biggest fish in the river, the paddlefish, which feeds on plankton and can grow as big as a man. The paddlefish is omitted from several lists of the watershed's fish, but I caught one below the dam at Caesar Creek Lake. I have also seen another caught, and got a good look at one swimming in clear water a few years ago.

The central stoneroller is the most common fish in the river comprising around forty percent of totals in several studies. Males dig spawning beds just upstream or downstream of riffles hence the name stonerollers. Usually just a plain grey minnow, males brighten up and grow tiny bumps called tubercles during breeding season. Found in both pools and riffles over a sandy or a gravel bottom, one thing stonerollers require is current. In a study of the fish community up and down the river, riffles in the middle section of the river such as at Stubbs Mills or Kings Mills averaged over forty fish species. Fish species collected that are sensitive to water pollution included stonecat madtom, mooneye, mimic shiner , river redhorse, hornyhead chub, river chub, silver shiner, rosyface shiner, black redhorse, northern madtom, mountain madtom, slenderhead darter, variegate darter and banded darter. At nearly all locations fish numbers were way up in a 2007 study over those found in 1998.

The story of how the water gets into the river might just be one of nature's greatest miracles. For you see, all the water seeping into the river through glacial deposits, every gallon that flows into the river from springs big and small, every drop of water that falls onto the river's watershed as rain, is part of an endless cycle so big it's almost impossible to describe. Every single drop of water on earth is part of this cycle. Every year over eighty thousand cubic miles of water is evaporated into the air from oceans, rivers, and lakes, (a number almost too big to have meaning, like billions and billions of stars). Plus, every living animal on earth adds water to the air with each breath, and through transpiration plants give off vast amounts of water.

All this water condenses into clouds and then falls to earth in the form of rain to begin the cycle anew. The amount of this water stored underground is vast also. It is estimated that under the United States the water supply is equal to ten years precipitation. Even underground the water is not lost from the cycle. Seeping downward, the water eventually reaches a layer of impervious rock and begins to move. Some resurfaces in springs like the famous Yellow Springs in the Little Miami's headwaters, or seeps directly into streams and rivers. The early explorers to the region were amazed at the Little Miami's clarity. Protected by seemingly endless woodlands and with no agricultural runoff, even in flood the river would run clear. Fed by an endless supply of dissolved organics from the great forest and with little silt, the aquatic life in the river must have been staggering. Even now, the beautiful Little Miami River is a jewel shining bright among the nation's rivers.

What's in the Box?

Nowadays with the fishing universe dominated by fishing for largemouth bass in lakes, there are literally thousands of lures to choose from. But the river fisherman uses an inline spinner or crankbait and often nothing else. And while these are great baits no one would seriously consider fishing a lake with only two baits. But the average river system is many times more complicated than a lake with a food chain so varied it's almost impossible to chart. Obviously the very act of wading a river limits the amount of tackle one can carry. But expanding past one or two lures can often mean the difference between catching little or a lot. I use a lightweight backpack that allows me to carry 4 or 5 of the cheap plastic lure boxes you can buy for a couple bucks at any big box store. Each has the capacity to hold 20 to 50 flies or lures. Here's a look at what I'm likely to have in my pack on any given trip.

I river fish the river sixty to seventy days a year most years, sometimes a lot more than that, and you won't ever catch me on the water without a three-inch plastic grub. If I'm wading and not carrying a lot of tackle I might have only a couple colors. One will be smoke metalflake. It just looks so much like a generic minnow in the water with just the right amount of flash, and I have caught so many fish with it over the years, I just have a lot of confidence throwing it. I'm also pretty big on the various orangish brown combinations, because I feel they look a lot like many of the darters and sculpins in the river. Bounced along the bottom, they also make an okay crawfish imitation.

If I'm sauger fishing in the winter, I'll probably be throwing some gawd-awful color, like lime green, chartreuse, or pink metalflake. Some days, the gaudier the better. I've seen days where if you get that right "glow" around your grub you will catch more sauger than anyone around. But just as likely they will want a subtle motor oil or shade of purple. I get more caught up in colors sauger fishing than any other fishing. For most fishing I'm a presentation first, color last, kind of guy. Seventy five percent of the time I fish a grub on an eighth ounce plain roundball jighead, but I will go up and down in weight. If I find fish feeding in a run but not on the bottom (white bass a lot, sometimes smallies), I'll go to a lighter weight to let the grub swim down the run on a tight line rather than hug the bottom. I also think sauger, in contrast to most other fish, actually like a bit of resistance when they hit. If I'm catching more sauger than bass, I'll fish a quarter-ounce jighead. I'll also go heavier in swifter deep water like below a low head dam.

I think you almost have to work at fishing a grub wrong. Just chucking it out and reeling it in will produce some fish, though most of the time I try to swim it slowly just off the bottom or let it sweep through a run on a tight line, also just off the bottom. In slower water like a hole or around a bridge abutment, I'll sometimes tight line the grub to the bottom, and bring it back in a series of lifts or slow sweeps. This is also a good way to pick up a nice channel cat or two. Some of the nicest channels I've caught have been on grubs. It certainly wakes you up to be smallmouth fishing, and tighten up on a ten pound catfish! That is one of the grub's main strengths. In a river like the Little Miami, you might catch any of seven or eight different species of fish on any given trip. I take a day or two every year and pour my own jigheads, which can save you a small fortune over time. In the last couple years I have also branched out to include other soft plastic bodies besides a grub body. Right up in the riffles and rocks, I might also throw a Jewel Sculpin. This guy is really just a grub with a big head and pectoral fins. In other words a great darter or madtom imitation. To imitate the shiners found in the pools I'll throw the River Rock Striker. This is a swim bait that has a great profile and action. I'm becoming a huge fan of this lure.

Like every river fisherman I carry some inline spinners. I use a slightly bigger inline spinner than most, throwing a 1/6 ounce model most of the time. I find a spinner to be the perfect prospecting lure and I'm most likely to tie one on when I want to cover some water. Spinners are at their best right above and below a riffle where the current's still moving fast. I think the flash elicits a reaction strike from bass that are up on the riffle to feed. I know inline spinners come in every color known to man but looking in my box, I find ninety- percent are mostly white or silver, the color of your average minnow. Lately I've been buying a few with some bright oranges and reds mixed in to imitate some of the darters that inhabit the fast water of the LMR. Recently, a plethora of small safety-pin style spinners have come on the market. While known mostly as a largemouth lure, in smaller sizes they are dandy for river fishing too. I use them like I would an inline spinner but also throw them to downed treetops, and other places you would likely snag or lose an inline spinner.

Another standard, that if you don't carry on the river people will look at you funny and ask just where are you from, is the floating minnow. The floating Rapala and Rebel minnow are the classics of this style of bait, and with good reason - they work extremely well. But nowadays there has been an explosion of minnow lures from dozens of makers that all perform wonderfully. I think one reason my color selection of inline spinners is so limited is that when trying to "match the hatch" with minnows I'm more likely to try with a minnow plug. I have one box stuffed with a couple dozen different sizes, shapes, and colors by a half dozen different makers. And I'm always buying new ones it seems. I'm going to go out on a limb though, and say the first one you should buy is a Rebel minnow 3 1/2 or 4 inches long in silver, because it looks so much like common minnows in the LMR, like the stoneroller. But I have seen times where a bigger minnow bait works wonders, especially at night.

One of the best features of minnow plugs is versatility. Twitched on top they make a great topwater plug and imitate a minnow in trouble better than anything I've ever seen. Twitch them, then pull the bait a foot or so under water, and just stop, letting it float back up to the surface like a minnow struggling. Just remember, when fishing one on top you must wait like you would with any topwater plug, before setting the hook. If you try to set it the instant a fish goes for the bait, you will miss half the fish, some days. An underwater, stop-and-go retrieve can often trigger strikes as well, and they make wonderful shallow water jerk baits, fished with slightly exaggerated pauses and sharper twitches on the retrieve.

These past few years, there has also been an explosion in the number of suspending minnow plugs.

A couple trips last year, a suspending minnow caught fish for me when I couldn't buy a strike on anything else. It lets you twitch and jerk a bait slowly underwater, and tease fish like a floating minnow does on top. A suspending minnow really shines in cold water too, letting you pause the lure for long periods of time, tempting even lethargic fish with the thought of an easy meal. Besides silvers and various shades of white and grey, I carry a few wilder color variations of minnow plugs, to match the brighter colors of darters. There are at least eleven species of darters in the LMR, and several other minnows that brighten considerably when spawning. For this reason I don't have a specific pattern I think is best. Probably best course is to try different patterns and just let the fish tell you what they want. Sampling has shown that the minnows inhabiting riffles can vary widely in color over just a few miles. Since the LMR is over hundred miles long, don't be afraid to experiment a bit with colors. Fishing with either flies or lures, I usually worry first about presentation, then size, then color. But some days, color can make a big difference.

One of the most popular lures on the Little Miami is the Rebel crawfish. These little guys are works of art with amazing attention to detail. I carry them in a few general colors that I try to match to any crayfish I see while wading. A fun lure to fish, they excel in deeper runs at the tails of riffles and in the heads of pools. As summer wears on, the young crayfish become large enough to interest smallmouth, and the Rebel craw really comes into its own. As the water cools, in fall, I begin to throw it less and less, as crawfish become less active themselves.

As time goes by I have become convinced the Rebel craw is more effective because it is just the right size and action, rather than an imitation that looks exactly like a crawfish.

As I said above, my priorities are usually presentation first, then size, then color. Sometimes, I'm just as likely to throw a small square-billed crankbait as well. A square- billed crankbait bounces off rocks and wood better than a round billed crankbait, and has a longer life span in the river. There is a variety of smaller square billed crankbaits that work great in the river. The two I fish the most are made by Rebel and Rapala, but several others would work just as well, I'm sure.

I carry several lipless crankbaits in my pack, more every year it seems. I use mostly smaller ones rather than the standard three-or four-inch largemouth lipless crankbait. But even the larger ones have their place at night. In the quiet and dark of night, the noise and vibration of a larger lipless crankbait seems to ring the dinner bell for several species of fish, from saugeyes to shovelheads. A lipless crankbait also does something I've found no other lure does; it appeals to the Buffalo (Ictiobus Bubalus, Smallmouth Buffalo). Sometimes mistaken for carp, the smallmouth buffalo features a flat face and large, silver scales running along the body, with a small-lipped, downturned mouth like a sucker, but lacking whisker-like mouth appendages common to carp. Native to the Ohio River, they can be found in freshwater creeks, rivers, and lakes, and are present in the LMR. Notably, Buffalo (the fish, not the mammal) reportedly were caught and eaten by members of the Lewis and Clark Expedition. I've found at night, it's not uncommon to hook a good size Buffalo on a large, lipless crankbait. I probably average hooking a Buffalo every other trip when I throw a lipless crankbait at night. At first I thought this was a fluke, as some fish were hooked outside the mouth. But it's happened too many times to be a coincidence. At most, only half are hooked inside the mouth, but the others were all hooked in the vicinity of the mouth, causing me to wonder if they are just batting at it, just to say who's boss. All I really know for sure is hooking a twenty pound Buffalo in the middle of a dark night will definitely get the old heart pounding. More and more I find myself throwing a chrome or silver lipless crankbait during the day; again, you never know what's going to hit it. Like the plastic grub, it catches everything that swims in the river. It's also a bait I have confidence in when the river's a bit off color or muddy because of those noisy rattles inside. In the lower reaches of the Little Miami a lipless crank is one of the best lures you can throw at a hybrid bass too.

In spring, once the water warms to the middle fifties, I begin to carry some topwaters. They are so fun to fish. I'll try to see how late in the fall I can still get a smallie to hit one. I carry several completely different types of topwater plugs. Some days one will seriously out fish the others. But river smallies, being the opportunists they are, most days will strike any well presented topwater popper or plug. Smaller, "walking the dog" plugs like the Heddon zara puppy will often trigger especially violent strikes, with the fish knocking the plug into the air before smashing it again. The trick is to keep walking the plug back, without stopping, until you feel the weight of the fish - easier said than done.

My favorite is an old Cotton Cordell plug that I don't think they even make anymore. It has a lead weight just in front of the rear treble to make the plug sit upright in the water. If you see any at a garage sale be sure and buy them, because the smallies love them. I also carry several different versions of poppers, the most famous example of being the Rebel Pop-r. In spring and again in fall when the fish are really biting, this noisy plug can often catch as many

fish as anything you can throw. Plus, poppers have a well-earned reputation as a big fish lure. I like them in the heads of pools, letting them float downstream popping them occasionally. They are also effective around any sort of wood. In fact, the largest rock bass I ever caught in the Little Miami hit a Pop-r thrown close to a log pile in a big eddy.

The Heddon Torpedo is a classic river topwater plug. This and other prop baits give you a completely different look and sound than other topwater plugs, somewhere between the loud "in your face" look of a popper, and the subtle teasing of a minnow plug. Bigger prop baits and jitterbugs also have a place when you're hitting the river at night. It's worth having one rigged up, to throw it once in a while during the night, while your catfishing some hole. Again, even at night, don't set the hook at the sound of the strike. Wait a split second until you feel the fish, and your hooking percentages will go way up. A buzzbait will often call up a hungry smallmouth as well, and many anglers swear by them. I also find a buzzbait to be a big fish lure when it comes to smallmouth in rivers, just as it is with largemouth in lakes and ponds.

If I were limited to only one lure to use in the LMR, I'd have to think a long time about making it a marabou jig. Out of fashion in today's high-tech fishing world, the marabou jig does several things extremely well. Fished slowly on the bottom, the marabou breathes, giving fantastic action on the slowest of retrieves. If you fish for bass in winter nothing (and I mean nothing) works better. You can use the old "float and fly" method and hang one below a floater. The filaments of marabou continue working as the lure hangs there, sometimes getting a bass to strike in water supposedly too cold for them to do so. Throughout the rest of the year marabou jigs worked slowly along the bottom will get strikes from everything that swims. You can even sight fish for tailing carp, like you would bonefish on the flats. I think a dark marabou jig imitates a hellgrammite, dragonfly nymph, or other big invertebrate better than anything. Of course you can also swim a light-colored one around brush for crappie, bass, sunfish, and rock bass, imitating a minnow as well. I try to fish as lightweight as I can, and still reach my target with an accurate cast. The lighter jigs swim better, and allow the marabou material to work better. Marabou jigs are also about the cheapest lures you can throw. They are staples for anyone fishing on a budget. It's one thing to lose a twenty-nine-cent jig, quite another to lose an eight-dollar crankbait.

Being also an avid hunter, I tie a lot of jigs with bucktail. I think bucktails excel as minnow imitations, especially when mixed with things like crystal flash or hi-viz. In fact I'm constantly scrounging new jig materials and have tied effective hair jigs with bear, fox, and coyote hair. I once met a guy on a trout stream who swore up and down he brought his pet dog home from the pound because its undercoat was just the right color cream for his favorite dry fly. And the last couple years, a favorite jig material has been craft fur. This fine "fur" moves almost as much as marabou but holds its shape a bit more in the water. It's gotten to the point; I can't pass a craft store or fly-tying shop without hauling home some new thing to add to the mix.

More basic river baits are soft plastics. You can fish something like a fluke or Slug-Go unweighted as a jerkbait. When you are retrieving one of these baits, do quick sharp jerks on a slightly slack line so the lure will dart freely and then glide after the jerk or twitch. While it is sinking, reel in some of your slack enough to allow for the next twitch but not enough to tighten the line and dampen its action.

A four-inch plastic worm rigged Texas style can be pitched into treetops and brush, and may tempt inactive bass out of cover on sunny bluebird days, when almost nothing else will work. Tubes, Texas-rigged, are also very effective river baits.

Bumped along the river bottom they make a great crayfish imitation. In areas without snags, a tube fished on the bottom, rigged on a lead jighead, is even more effective. I sort of picture this tube as a crayfish imitation, while a curly-tailed grub fished off the bottom as a minnow imitation. Many fishermen only carry one or the other, but carry a few of both grubs and tubes to cover a broader section of the food chain.

Another fine crayfish imitation is a skirted jig. Several studies have shown smallmouth, even large ones, prefer smaller crayfish. That being said, I'll fish what amounts to smaller versions of the traditional "jig and pig", favored by largemouth fishermen everywhere. Sometimes that just means taking a pair of scissors or a sharp knife to the rubber skirt of a traditional jig. I'll tip that with a small twin-tailed grub. One important thing to remember when fishing a skirted jig along the bottom is to become an intent line watcher. While some days bass will really bop the jig, on others the only sign of a strike may be twitch of the line. Don't think of the skirted jig just as a heavy cover lure when fishing for smallmouth in the river. While these baits excel in heavy cover, smallmouth are wired a bit differently than largemouth. They cruise open water a bit more, and may attack a skirted jig in the open, a bit away from heavy cover. And don't just picture wood and rock as structure. In the river, think of structure as including current seams and eddies as well.

One interesting study on smallmouth eating preferences involved introducing smallmouth into an aquarium with madtoms in it. The madtoms froze and the smallmouth gobbled them up. But if crayfish were also in the tank along with the madtoms, a much higher percentage of madtoms survived. Researchers were not sure how to interpret this. Did the crayfish distract the smallmouth a split second longer enabling some of the madtoms to escape, or were the madtoms helped by the crawfish behavior to recognize, "Hey! There's a bass!".

I often can't sleep at night, a product of years spent working the late shift I guess. I'll turn on the Outdoor Channel and watch those guys dressed like Nascar drivers fishing exotic locations with $30,000 bass boats loaded with more gear than my father's old bait shop had stocked on all the shelves. That kind of fishing is fun, I admit. But there is no doubt in my mind, you can have a great trip, possibly the best of the year, fitting everything you need in a shirt pocket.

All you really need are three or four basic pieces of terminal tackle to catch fish almost any time you fish a river like the Little Miami. First off, get a pack or two of baitholder hooks in size two or four. You can substitute a similar size hook of another style, but baitholders are available almost everywhere, and work great. You might want to add a pack of treble hooks in size eight, for carp. Next get a pack or two of barrel swivels, and some egg sinkers and you're set. Rigging is simplicity itself. The egg sinker is slid onto the line, and a barrel swivel is tied into the line about a foot above the hook.

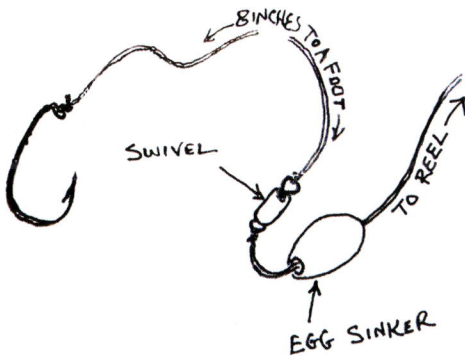

This is ideally fished on a medium spinning outfit with six-or eight-pound test line. The rig is then tossed out, the rod set in a forked stick, and a pebble from the riverbank placed on the line so you can leave the bail open without the line being carried away by the current. Oh, and don't forget the bait. It really helps to bait the hook if you're serious about catching fish. Nightcrawlers will be just fine for nearly all species. More than the tackle, the key to catching at least some fish every trip depends on location. Where you want to set up is in a well-defined hole just below a nice riffle. Right where the current first begins to slow. If there is an eddy and a deep pocket, even better. Too many people fishing bait in

the river just set up in the middle of a long slow hole away from the riffle, cover, or the main current. Most of the time, this is a recipe for catching little or nothing. Thread on a nightcrawler and fish below a good riffle, and you might catch just about anything in the river, from all the catfish species, to the occasional bass or carp. In addition, nowadays you are just about guaranteed to catch a freshwater drum or two (or ten). Anytime water temperature rises above the upper fifties, a nightcrawler on light line just about guarantees some drum. Switch to minnows and you just might catch a nice sauger, white bass, or flathead. Baiting up with crayfish in the two or three-inch range can also catch just about anything that swims. Change the baitholder out with the treble hook and bait up with a dough ball made of Wheaties and hamburger, and you're set for channel cats and carp. Trust me, catching a half-dozen five-or six-pound carp on light spinning tackle will change the way you look at these guys forever.

I must admit my favorite way to fish the river is wading, casting for smallmouth bass with flies or lures. But even on these trips, I often throw a dozen nightcrawlers in the daypack. About midday, I'm ready for a break and stop at a nice riffle, and throw a live-baited rig out, while I eat a sandwich. It's amazing just how often this "break" produces the most memorable fish of the day.

In the heart of winter every year I start on rebuilding my fly selection for the coming year. In addition to the old standbys, I hit the Orvis store at the Dayton Mall and try to reverse engineer some of their flies. To me, they have the best smallie fly selection around and some weirdly cool flies you just can't find anywhere else. Like, for example, my favorite crayfish fly, May's Clearwater Crayfish.

I love this fly. It has everything I'm looking for in a crayfish fly. Good color. It sinks like a rock. It has rubber legs for movement, and only a suggestion of claws. Study after study shows smallmouth prefer crayfish with small claws, or no claws for that matter. This guy is pretty close to the perfect crayfish fly in my book. I fish it on a short line, usually across and down in riffles and runs. Other flies I fish in this same manner are weighted stonefly nymphs, and two other weirdly wonderful flies, the Conehead Rubber Bugger and Shultzy's Red Eyed Leech.

I think both the Conehead Rubber Bugger and the Shultzy look a little bit like a whole slew of stuff smallmouth are looking to eat in runs and riffles. They slightly resemble everything from a darter to some kind of big nymph to even a little crayfish. At any riffle on the Little Miami there's going to be a dozen kinds of dark and rusty-colored little fish in and among the rocks as well as a list of invertebrates as long as your arm. I think a smallmouth up on a riffle sees a lot of different stuff and isn't about to be as selective as a fish in slower water. That's why I really go for these generalized creepy crawly flies.

When fishing pools for smallmouth I try to imitate shiners more than anything else. Both the LMR and GMR have about a dozen shiner species and in most stretches of calmer water they are far and away more common than anything else. I like unweighted shiner flies because shiners are usually more active high in the water column and don't hug the bottom like riffle minnows and darters.

As a general rule, I try to fish heavier, weighted flies, and darker flies the closer I get to the riffle, and lighter color flies the farther I am into the deeper pool. This is in a general way following the pattern of the dozens of little baitfish in the river. But there are exceptions to the rule. There are so many variables that this only gives you a place to start. If the fish aren't biting, don't be afraid to experiment. The food chain in smallmouth streams is more complicated than just about any other kind of water. If someone tells you they know exactly what's going on down there at any one time, you know how little they really do know. Sometimes I think we catch fish in spite of our best theories. We think we are catching smallmouth feeding on crayfish, and they are actually feeding on rainbow darters, flushed out of the rocks by crawfish too big for smallmouth to eat; or any of a hundred other scenarios that might be going on at any given time.

Of course you also must have some topwater flies. Topwater fly fishing in streams is fishing at its very finest. I throw deer-hair bugs a lot just because I have a huge supply of deer hair from years of bow hunting, but a Sneaky Pete might be a better choice, if you're only going to buy or tie one. A Sneaky Pete lets you fish the slicks in the tail of pools without getting waterlogged like a deer-hair bug, and is just as effective as deer hair in quiet water. Some days, a deer-hair bug or Sneaky Pete can be simply deadly. Another fly I fish on the surface is a Marabou Muddler. I know it's a streamer, but dressed with just a bit of floatant, it fishes in the film. I call it fishing it soggy, not wet or dry. It's exciting just like topwater fishing, and just as visual.

Many of our rivers hold an amazing bunch of fish that are largely overlooked by fishermen. Hard to catch, hard fighting and growing to nice sizes, you would think these fish would be all the rage, but they suffer from either bad press or no press. Even worse is their name: "suckers". After all, don't "permit" have the same downturned mouth, are hard to catch on a fly, and grow to roughly the same sizes? But permit are saltwater flats glamour fish, and suckers are . . . well, "suckers"! Many species are highly intolerant of pollution, and used by biologists like canaries in the coal mine when it comes to water quality. Many suckers have special adaptations such as reduced swim bladders to help them stay in place in swift riffles. The hog sucker even has a head shaped to use like spoilers on race cars to create a down force to hold itself in place in the moving current. And the hog sucker, like many suckers, uses big pectoral fins like those on a darter or madtom to brace itself in place on bottom in a riffle's swift water.

Suckers eat algae and small invertebrates and will hit a nymph if you can present it right in front of them. They will not chase a nymph, though. The key is to present the fly right on the sucker's nose. I find the best way to do this is with stealthy wading and a high-stick, short-line nymphing technique just like you would use for trout in a swift riffle or run.

Sometimes in clear water, if you wade carefully enough, you can spot and cast at the fish you are presenting the fly to. But most times, sunlight and turbulence on the water hides the fish, no matter how clear the water is. With this in mind, always wear polarized sunglasses. You will not likely spot fish without these. When casting, work the stream thoroughly even though you have not spotted any fish, keeping in mind the fish will not turn and chase the fly. As I have stated, a good presentation seems much more important than the particular fly pattern. Any good beadhead will get bit, if you put it on a feeding sucker's nose. I tie some brighter versions of my standard beadhead nymphs to make them more noticeable to a feeding sucker.

When fly casting for suckers, I find a long fly rod works better than a shorter one, as it gives you more range to short-line a nymph and a longer follow. A five-or six-weight 9 foot fly rod is just about right. Suckers sometimes are too large to land on three or four-weight fly rods. Five and six weights are good. Seven-weights and up are probably overkill.

When short-lining a nymph, you do not need a strike indicator, but on longer casts, use an indicator up the line just a little farther than the water is deep. Setting the indicator this deep will insure your nymphs are on the bottom, where they need to be. Plan on losing quite a few to snags. If you are not bumping and hooking bottom every now and again, your nymph is not deep enough.

Best I can tell, there are sixteen species of suckers in the Little Miami River. Some, like the white sucker, are very common.

Others, like the endangered blue sucker are among the rarest fish in the river.

If you are lucky enough to hook a blue sucker, handle it carefully. Get it in quickly, rather than fighting it to exhaustion. Snap a quick picture if you must, then promptly set it free, making sure it is in good enough shape to swim off under its own power. Watch it awhile making sure it will not roll over and go belly up. If it is not stable enough to release, cradle it gently in your hands in good moving water, with the fish pointing upstream against the current, and move the tail gently back and forth in a slow swimming motion. Most times, strength will return in a minute or two, and the fish will swim off under its own power. This is good advice for all fish you are releasing. All fish are an important part of the ecosystem and should be handled with care.

Some other non-traditional fly rod species that will hit a fly include carp and Buffalo. Both will eat the same flies as suckers, with good presentation of the fly to the fish being much more important than the pattern. Below is a picture of my fly box that displays the type of flies that are attractive to suckers and carp. Several of these are good trout baits too.

Matching the Hatch

There are literally thousands of imitations of everything that bass feed on in lakes, but check the box of the typical stream fisherman and you're lucky to find much more than a half dozen different lures, and some of these are more at home in still water. There are some inline spinners like the roostertail, and minnow plugs and the Rapala that do a good job imitating minnows and chubs that live in the stream's pools and backwaters, but that's about it. Small fish that inhabit the riffles and runs of our smallmouth streams and rivers have been completely ignored, for often these look nothing like the silvery minnows of the backwaters.

In my home water, the Little Miami River, there are no fewer than 13 species of darters and five species of madtoms that live in riffles. All these little fish have strong pectoral fins to hold their place among the rocks in the swift current. When viewed from above (as would a foraging smallmouth looking for food) these pectoral fins are a very noticeable feature of most darters and madtoms. These little fish seemingly come in an endless variety of colors ranging from quite dull to brighter than any aquarium fish. Many darter species also change color during breeding season to attract a mate. I've tried to come up with a few simple ways to imitate these little-known but important members of the river's food chain.

Using acrylic paints, leadhead jigs can be painted to give you options during a day's fishing. A coat of clear finger nail polish protects the paint from

chipping on the rocky stream bottom. A round ball jig best imitates madtoms and pointier types more closely resemble most darter species. Having a few of both types in a variety of colors gives you more options to experiment with on the water.

Take a grub or plastic worm and cut a triangle out of the tail with scissors. This triangle is then threaded on the jighead ahead of another grub to represent the prominent pectoral fins of your darter or madtom. Often there are a few species on every riffle with pectoral fins that are brightly tinged with color and using a triangle cut out of a grub that contrasts in color with the grub used for the body of the jig can make a big difference. As there are often multiple species of darters and madtoms on the riffle together, the smallmouth are used to feeding on a wide variety of colors. I carry several colors feeding on a wide variety of colors. I carry several colors of triangles already cut out in my tackle box and a variety of colored grubs. By mixing and matching different triangles with different grub bodies you can experiment to find the combination that works best on any day. The main constants are size and the prominent pectoral fins. I almost always fish a three-inch grub on an eighth ounce jighead and just vary colors. Darters and madtoms spend almost their entire lives among the rocks of a stream's riffles and runs, the same places smallmouth move in to feed. Fish your imitation along the bottom in short, quick motions or let it sweep along the bottom in the current, as these little fish do not swim up high in the water column or in schools, but as the name implies dart from rock to rock. These little guys are almost never caught in traditional minnow traps but are only seen by using a seine right among the rocks of the riffle.

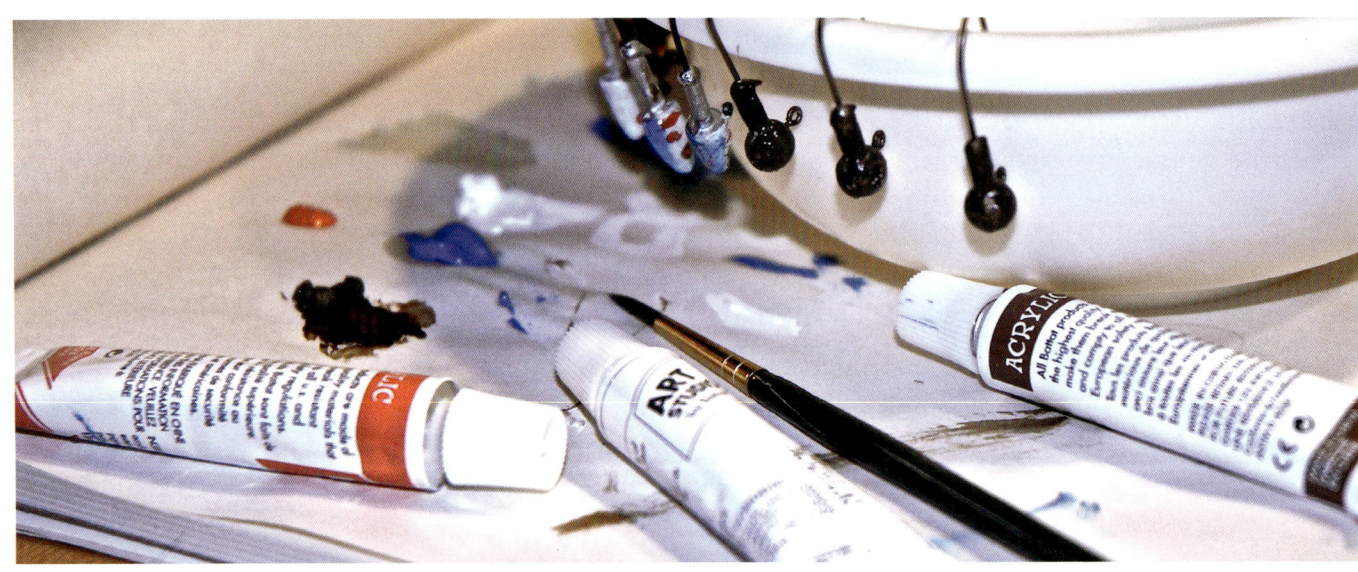

Another resident you will seine out of these riffles, and a main reason smallmouth love to feed there, is the crayfish. While there are some great crayfish imitations out there, such as the jig and pig, these are mostly just too big to imitate the small crayfish that stream smallmouth love. A modified double-tailed grub makes one of the best imitations of these little craws I know of. I first use the jighead like a crochet needle to pull living rubber through the grub's body to make legs.

I then trim these to length with scissors.

Just like darters, crayfish can vary widely in color so it pays to have different combinations of bodies and legs. Sometimes a bit of bright orange or red living rubber can be key in triggering smallmouth when they are in a picky mood. Finding out more about the things that smallmouth feed on in your stream and adding baits that imitate them can add new dimensions to your stream fishing arsenal.

A warm water river like the Little Miami holds a tremendous variety of life when compared to a cold water trout stream. The fish in the Little Miami are much more likely to eat a fly just because it looks like something good to eat rather than an exact copy of a specific insect or fish specie.

I try to carry good generic flies like the parachute adams that might imitate any of a dozen things on the water at any one time. For smallmouth a generic stonefly/hellgrammite pattern cast upstream and across and allowed to tumble back like an insect caught in the current is often a top producer. Early and late in the day, a deer hair bug fished in the slick at the tail of a pool or around structure can produce exciting strikes. I like a slightly smaller bug than is normally thrown in ponds for largemouth. And I really like my smaller version, the googly, for non-stop action.

Here's my recipe for tying the googly.

First, you tie in a tail of fox or squirrel and a piece of tinsel.

Then you wrap the tinsel forward till it covers about 60% of the hook shank and tie it in.

Next tie in wings from a saddle. I like grizzly but use whatever I have left over from tying dry flies.

Then you take some deer hair and loop the thread over it twice. As you pull the thread taut you release the hair with your fingers, letting it flare and spin around the hook shank.

Repeat tying in bunches of deer hair till you fill up the hook shank completely.

Tie off the thread and trim the deer hair.

Epoxy on your eyes and you're done!

Smallmouth Bass

The most sought after fish in the Little Miami River is the smallmouth bass.

The smallmouth bass gets its name from the fact that the back end of the lower jaw does not extend past the eye, as the jaw of a largemouth does. Their preferred water temperature is 68-70 degrees F, cooler than that of the largemouth bass. Spawning activity begins in the spring when water temperatures reach 60 degrees F or more. The male builds a nest in quiet water, usually near shore, or downstream from an obstruction that causes a break in the current. Since the male will guard the eggs and the newly hatched fry, the nest is never far from deep water, or cover, where he can retreat when frightened.

Smallmouth eggs are larger than those of the largemouth bass, and hatch in roughly three days. Then the newly hatched fry hide in the gravel at the bottom of the nest for a few or more days. After that the fry hang around the nest for a few more days before they begin to disperse. Until then, these tiny fry are guarded by the adult male, who hangs around, keeping a watchful eye on things.

At first the fry eat tiny crustaceans, but soon begin to add insects and fish to their diet as they grow in size.

Smallmouth bass mature at age three and a very old one might live to be 10 to 12 years old. The usual smallmouth seen by anglers is 10 to 14 inches long, and weighs less than three pounds. The world record smallmouth was caught in Dale Hollow Lake in July of 1955 by David Hayes. It weighed 11 pounds 15 ounces! He was trolling a model 300 Bomber in deep water. The Ohio record smallmouth was caught on a jigging spoon in Lake Erie in 1993 by Randy Van Dam (yeah he's Kevin Van Dam's brother) and weighed a staggering 9lb 8 ounces. The world record largemouth bass is just a tad under twice as big as the world record smallmouth and that is a good indication of the difference in average size of the two bass species. But the smallmouth has a well-earned reputation as the hardest fighting fish so there is a surprise for everyone who catches one for the first time.

Smallmouth also have a reputation for being moody, cantankerous fellows that won't hit anything one minute then smash the heck out of your bait the next cast. I like them a lot. Smallmouth bass thrive in streams with gravel or rock bottoms with a visible current such as the Little Miami River. Smallmouth bass outnumber largemouth bass in most streams and rivers in Ohio. In southern Ohio smallmouth are out numbered by spotted bass in some of the largest rivers such as the Muskingum, Scioto, and Ohio Rivers. Smallmouth bass are common in Lake Erie, which might just be the best smallmouth fishery in the world. They can also be found in some of Ohio's reservoirs, especially those that are deeper and clearer with steep drop offs and rocky shorelines, but smallmouth are almost never as numerous as largemouth in Ohio's lakes. In the LMR any smallmouth over 3 pounds is certainly worth snapping a photo of before releasing. Any smallie over 4 pounds is probably the catch of a lifetime. In thirty years of fishing the LMR, I've only managed to land a couple smallmouth over 5 pounds from the Little Miami. Although the Little Miami is prime smallmouth habitat, and small and medium sized fish abound, their presence and numbers are not to be taken for granted. The very nature of stream and river habitat means there will be occasional terrible spawns caused by flooding. Therefore, every conscientious, ethical fisherman should practice catch and release with all smallmouth bass, especially those rare giants which are tremendous egg producers. I'm not against fish fries, just smallmouth bass fish fries.

Locating Fall Smallmouth

The thing I probably get the most questions about in all of my fishing is how I locate bass in the fall. Fishermen say they constantly hear how good smallmouth bass fishing is in the fall, but that they just can't catch them or they are only catching dinks. Well here's how I locate smallies in the fall. Smallmouth migrate to the best possible places they can find to spend the winter. This may only be hundreds of yards or it might be ten miles or more.

One study (Ross Langhurst and Dean Schenike of the Wisconsin DNR) tracked some smallmouth that migrated over 70 miles (!) but there are good wintering holes every ten miles or less over the length of the LMR. This migration is triggered by length of day. Dr. Mark Ridgeway, a research scientist for the Ontario Ministry of Natural Resources, found that a smallmouth migration away from classic summer habitat begins, each year, within a week to 10 days of the autumnal equinox in September. This means that day length, not water temperature, is the reason for smallmouth bass fall movements. But there are two parts to the puzzle. Whether or not they then bite is related to water temperature. When the water temperature drops to 60 degrees and below that seems to be a trigger point. From then till the river hits 50 degrees the smallmouth are in overdrive feeding the strongest they do all year. So the great fishing lasts as long as the water stays above about 52. If that's a week, it's a week. If it's a month then the fishing is great for a month. So between the smallmouth migration and water temps you need a couple things you might not have used all year.

The number one tool for finding smallmouth bass wintering holes in the LMR is a good on-line satellite-mapping site like Google Maps. You're looking for big bends and deep eddies with complex structure nearby. You want the deepest, biggest holes you can find. Some of these may be right downtown, or in other locations considered "fished out" during the summer. This does not matter, because you are fishing for smallmouth bass that are making their fall migration. They may have come from miles away to get to that special fall and winter location. Sometimes you just have to make a list of possibilities, then head out to find them. Like I said, the bass will migrate as far as it takes. That means you can't be thinking of your favorite summer spots and concluding, "Well, maybe this is good enough." You may need to go farther than you think.

Until the water actually hits 50 to 53 the bass might be nearby, but not yet right in that wintering hole. They will instead be somewhere on the first two or three riffles either upstream or down feeding like gangbusters. The best places I know have both the deep complex structure and a really good hard bottomed riffle, with no silt between the feeding area and the hole, though in one case may be 150 yards or so between the two.

A thermometer is a great tool for figuring out where things are. Above 60, you can expect bass to be in transition between summer and fall patterns. The equinox falls on September 22, 23, or 24 every year. On any other day of the year, the Earth's axis tilts a little away from or towards the sun, but on the equinox the Earth's axis tilts neither away from nor towards the sun. So sometime within a week of that, expect them to come pouring into those fall feeding riffles, depending on temps. Not every smallmouth migrates at exactly the same time so you can still catch bass elsewhere in the river as they stop to feed while migrating, but the real action will be in those good riffles close to wintering holes starting about the second week in September, and getting better and better, if the weather cooperates, until the water cools below 50 to 53 degrees. There is an easy way to find fall smallmouth when the river is between 60 and 55. "If you ain't catching them, you ain't on 'em." If the elements described above are in place, they will most certainly be feeding, and biting the best they will all year. After the river cools below 50

you have to fish slooow, down in the deep wintering holes to get much action. Sometimes a warm day will warm things a degree or two and you can sometimes catch a smallmouth or two on a hair jig fished almost motionless under a float. Just let the current swirl it around the hole adding as little movement to the lure as possible. This can result in some of the best fish of the year, but it also results in many fishless days as well.

Finding and Catching Twenty-Inch Smallmouth

So you really want a 20-inch smallmouh bass - a true trophy; from a stream or river; not Canada, not Lake Erie, not Dale Hollow. Try this approach for a year and you will catch one.

First off, there are a couple important, fundamental things you need to know and believe in, to buy in to this strategy. These are important, and they are proven to be true. One is that smallmouth bass basically are extreme homebodies.

In summer, they do not move from their chosen defined home area. Catch a big rainbow trout out of the best spot in a trout stream, knock it in the head and eat it. If you come back in two weeks another big trout has taken its spot. That isn't the case with smallmouth bass. Except for spawning time and their migration to their wintering holes, a big smallmouth will live its entire life in the same one or two pools of the river, returning to their same summer place, year after year! Study after study shows this. How is this important in finding big smallmouth? Well, it means you have to find a stretch of river where a big smallmouth can live for seven or eight years at least, without somebody knocking it in the head and eating it. From most studies I've seen, smallmouth will use a defined riffle as a boundary, and often will never cross the boundary and leave their summer range, except to migrate in fall. NEVER! Hence, in summer a really sharp, strong, across-the-river riffle will be home for two completely different populations of mature smallmouth; one upstream and one downstream of the defined boundary created by the riffle. These mature smallmouth will not cross from one side to the other side of the riffel, except when they leave for their winter holes.

So where to fish?

Start at a familiar access point to the river - a stretch everyone fishes. They won't be there, because the nice mature ones have been removed by all the folks who fish there all the time. They are gone, and other mature smallmouth will not have moved in, no matter how good the water looks. You go either upstream or downstream from that fished out location, (either in person or on Google maps), until you find another well defined riffle - one that goes all the way across the river, in a place that is not heavily fished. That is the place you are looking for. That riffle is the boundary separating two distinct populations of mature smallmouth. The fish above that is a completely separate population from the ones below, and both are entirely separate from the population of mature smallmouth population that have been hammered and taken out, back in the convenient, easy access stretch.

Follow your newly discovered well-defined riffle pool, all the way to the next well- defined boundary. No access points in between? No easy water to get to? Now you're getting somewhere. Between those two boundaries, is your best specific place to fish to locate mature, big smallies. They will be there, and they will not cross those boundaries. You may find them right at the boundary line itself, or somewhere else in the area between that boundary and the next one. Just understand that one side of a riffle might be trophy water and the other side, just full of small fish, but without any mature ones, even though they are just thirty yards apart. Odd, isn't it? Strange, but true. I'm not sure any other river fish behaves just like this. Shovelheads are homebodies too, but in times of high water will range wildly and repopulate fished out holes.

A hole where the big smallies are fished out is just

that, fished out. It might be chock full of smaller fish, but the presence of these immature ones is no indication as far as big fish are concerned. So here is your strategy. You create a list of spots. These will be very specific target spots, between good (not overfished) boundary lines. You do this for as many different stretches of the river as you can. The Little Miami River has numerous such stretches. Some are remote, in the middle of nowhere, hard to get to. Others may be located adjacent to private property lined with houses that are not home to fishermen, or at least not home to fishermen that don't keep fish.

Lets face it, even kayak fishermen most often hit areas where they can launch and land easily, and take long, all-day floats thru hard-to-reach stretches rarely. Plus most of these guys are catch and release guys, who will not likely remove mature fish from these good locations. It really doesn't matter how remote or difficult a stretch is to get to. The key is that defined boundary to separate it from the easy access fished out places.

In that stretch, we have found where we want to fish for those mature, bigger smallmouth bass. I'm a firm believer that the biggest baddest smallmouth will take the best spot. Why do smallmouth in lakes school according to size? Because the bigger ones are mean predators, and the littler guys avoid them. In a river, that means the big bass, the one we are trying to catch, takes the best spot. Some spots are obvious. Other times the best spot is not obvious. Maybe something out of the norm is going on and that fish is cruising back and forth below a riffle nabbing stonerollers that are spawning or any of a dozen other scenarios.

Like I said, maybe your big fish is off doing something else that day. But if you come back time after time to the best three or four spots in that stretch and fish them over and over, eventually you are going to find that fish at home. Find three or four potentially good stretches of river defined by specific boundaries at each end. Then find the best spots in each of those potential stretches.

Now the hard part. Fish those. Fish them in the rain. Fish them in the middle of the night. Fish them at dawn. Fish them in the middle of the day. Fish them till you know them by heart - until you can close your eyes and picture every tree, every rock, every nuance of current even though you're home in bed. You're probably going to catch half as many fish as you did when you just got in the river and waded, throwing an inline spinner everywhere that looked even halfway fishy. You're probably not going to catch even half as many. A quarter or a third is more like it. But you're eventually going to catch THE fish. Like I said it's all about catching just that one really big fish.

Most of time that best spot is going to be some sort of seam. Somewhere there is a well defined line between currents of differing speeds. Maybe a creek mouth that has a pocket of dead water with the main river current creating a line across it; rubble from an old dam; a rock bar or a riffle. Any of a hundred different things may create that magical line. Sometimes it's all hidden underwater, but often you can see that sharp line drawn on the surface where the seam is. If you find one of these, fish it until you're blue in the face.

Then on the next trip, hit it hard again, and the next trip, again. Sometimes, in some flows, under some conditions, that seam will become the best spot that day, and your big fish will be there. Maybe not today, or tomorrow, but someday. Never ever pass up a seam in your chosen stretches of river. Even if you have been skunked there five trips in a row. Who knows, trip six, seven or eight just might be the one. You will eventually catch that 20-incher, and another, and another. It's repeatable year after year.

Those Other Bass- THE WHITE BASS RUN

Sometime in April, the riffles of the lower sections of the Little Miami will fill up with white bass. These guys are partaking in their annual spawning run up the Little Miami from the Ohio River. A few of them will remain in the Little Miami all year and I've caught them upstream in the river's upper reaches. But only on the lower river below Milford or Terrace Park can you count on enjoying the spectacle that is the white bass run.

So far the annual run has managed to fly under the radar for most fishermen, and fishing the run isn't as congested as some other, better-known runs. But don't let that fool you. Days with fish counts in the hundreds are not rare at the height of the white bass run on the Little Miami River. Seek out any riffle or strong current break to hold fish. Throw something flashy like an inline spinner or silvery crankbait a couple inches long and by the end of the day the paint will literally be eaten off of it. I find deeper runs and fast bends tend to hold the bigger fish. During the height of the run you might catch several white bass big enough to qualify for Ohio's Fish Ohio award program in a single outing. It's a truly world class fishery.

At the same time the white bass are running expect to find a few hybrid stripers mixed in. Hybrid striped bass are a silvery deep fish, similar to white bass. Stripes along the sides and back are distinct, usually broken, with several extending to the tail. Teeth on the base of the tongue are arranged in two parallel patches. There are a few big hybrids in the river in spring, and again in the fall. A close mouthed group of hybrid fanatics stalk the lower LMR religiously. You need a reel with a high quality drag to land one of these guys. Imagine a ten-pound smallmouth hitting your lure and you have a good approximation of the fight of a hybrid striper.

Once in a blue moon you might catch a pure strain striper in the Little Miami but they are very rare compared to the other silver bass. Hybrid striper action is often feast or famine with fish blowing up everywhere around you one second and then nothing the next. Hybrids are nomads roaming large distances in search of their prey, primarily gizzard shad. Follow the bait and you will eventually find the fish. Hybrids are even more concentrated in just the lower reaches on the Little Miami than even white bass. The furthest upstream I have caught one is South Lebanon and that was a rare event. Fast current and gravely sandy riffles seem to produce better than the rocky cobbled riffles that smallmouth prefer.

Saugfishes

I'm no expert on saugthings (sauger, saugeye, walleye), but I do fish for them a lot come winter and people ask about them more than anything else; so here's how I do it. First off, the last thing I want do in winter is worry if there are any fish where I'm fishing to see my bait. In summer there are fish spread through the whole river, in winter that isn't the case. Find a complicated stretch, even if you have to drive ten minutes farther, it's worth it. I want an island with water pouring around both sides, or at least a big S-curve, a deep run, a riffle and DEEP WATER all in close proximity. Yeah that's a lot to ask for, but if I fish through all that, I know I

will have shown my lure to at least a few fish. I've read where sauger may migrate a hundred miles in big rivers in winter. It stands to reason they will migrate 5 or 6 in a small river like the LMR to select a great stretch of river. If I'm fishing the Great Miami for winter saugs I'm fishing below one of the dams. It's simply better below the dams. So there's no reason to go anywhere else. Ninety percent of the time I'm throwing a three inch grub. Not just any grub but a gawdawfull butt ugly one. Try pink or orange or neon green, the brighter and gaudier the better most days. Try to get a "glow" going around your bait. Sometimes they like neon pink over red with gold metal flake. Color matters some days, even if your fishing some horrid color no live fish has ever seen before. Bring a hook-sharpening file, because the rocks will do a number on your hook. Expect to lose a lot of baits. I lose *hundreds* in the course of a year.

The other lure I fish is a sinking or suspending minnow. Once in a while it will out-produce the grub. Everyone I talk to says minnows on a jighead will out-produce both, but I hate to fool with live bait in the cold. Concentrate on slack water right up against current most of the time, but expect to try everywhere. I've caught them anywhere as long as a deep hole was close by riffle or the dam. Some days you just feel a mushy weight instead of a strike, so set the hook on weight in the winter.

I also find that sauger sometimes have the odd habit of only wanting the bait presented one way. Just because you didn't get a strike fishing upstream doesn't mean the same lure won't get a strike fished downstream.

Another trick I see almost no one doing in winter, is fishing after dark. Saugeye, walleyes, sauger all are strongly nocturnal fish. Fishing where no one will see you and call the cops on the crazy man may enable you to do very well at night in the winter. And that's it. I'm sure there's other ways to catch them but that's how I go about it. ... fish ugly lures for an ugly fish that doesn't fight all that well while freezing your tail off possibly even in the middle of the night. Fishing doesn't end in winter, if you're bold enough and dressed for it.

Catfish

I looked up just as Dan's rod bowed into a half-circle with line screaming off the reel. Ten minutes later I snapped his photo with a twenty-pound shovelhead. I watched as he released the fish and I started back down the bank. I hadn't made it thirty yards when I heard a whoop and turned around. There he was fast into another big fish, his rod bent double once *again*. It turned out to be another shovelhead just bigger than the first. The most amazing thing about these two nice fish wasn't that they were caught on back-to-back casts. It was that neither was caught on live bait, or any sort of traditional catfish bait for that matter. They say that seeing is believing, and I listened intently as Dan told me about the big cats he had been taking regularly on crankbaits. Now almost everyone who fishes has caught an accidental cat or two on lures. But this was something different; something I had to try. And after experimenting with this new way of catfishing for a year now, I can tell you it works. In the last twenty trips alone, I've caught fifty-six shovelheads ranging from five to thirty pounds, plus at least that many bonus fish such as channel cat, smallmouth and drum.

The only lure I throw when trying to catch a shovel-head is a lipless crankbait. There are dozens of versions on the market; the flat, pointed on the ends, lipless crankbates, filled with BB's are great. And the nice thing about it is shovelhead don't seem to care which one you use, so long as it's loud - the louder the better. In fact, it seems the cheaper ones might just be the best. Wal-Mart and Bass Pro both sell a discount crankbait in the two-dollar range that seems to work as well as anything. If you pick it up and shake it in your hand, and it sounds like your playing maracas in a bad mariachi band, it's probably perfect. I don't really worry much about color, either. Shovelhead have small eyes. They don't use eyesight as their main sense the way a bass or a trout does. Shovelheads rely much more on two other senses; smell and sound detection. You see, catfish are particularly alert to vibrations in the water, making them able to feed on the darkest nights and in muddy water. When a big cat is cruising the shallows at night, hungry for dinner, that big vibrating crankbait may not smell like dinner, but if it moves and sounds alive, an aggressive cat will nail it. I guess the future of this kind of fishing might be a crankbait that also smells like a shad, or some other small fish.

As generations of noodlers will tell you, shovelheads spend a great deal of time backed up under heavy cover like an underwater ledge, a log, or a tangle of tree roots. But shovelheads are ferocious predators that prefer to kill their food rather than scavenge off the bottom like other catfish species.

Late at night that shovelhead that spent all day in an undercut bank is now out on the prowl looking for an unsuspecting meal. The key to catching them consistently is finding places where big cats congregate when searching for a meal. The best spots I've found are just below a low head dam in a small to medium size river. The dam concentrates food, and often has a large population of hungry shovelhead cruising around, hoping for a meal. A dam in a smaller river usually is not so huge that it has the powerful currents of a big dam on a big river like the Ohio or Mississippi. While these big river dams hold lots of huge cats, most fisherman rely on two or three ounce lead weight just to keep their bait in place, meaning getting your crankbait down to the fish is almost impossible. The big dams can also be dangerous to fish near. But in a smaller river, you can sometimes cover the water completely, getting your crankbait down as needed, insuring a hungry cat will eventually encounter and hopefully devour it. It's been my experience a cat will cruise the whole area below a dam, searching for food, so you might hook up anywhere though a couple areas seem to produce the best. I try to throw right up against the dam if possible, as there is often a nice cat or two, right where the water pours over. If the dam throws up a rock bar below the scour hole, pay particular attention to it, especially late at night. Minnows often come up extremely shallow there to escape predators and the shovelheads follow. It's not uncommon late at night to hook up almost right under the rod tip. When a twenty-pound fish smashes your lure at four in the morning right under your nose, be expecting it. It would be easy to be startled so bad you drop your rod!

I try to form a mental picture of the river bottom below the dam, and keep the rattlebait moving just fast enough to tick the bottom every now and then. My basic retrieve is a lot like you might use if swimming a jig or plastic grub right along the bottom. In the deeper water of the pool, count or time the bait's descent, making sure it achieves sufficient depth, before beginning your retrieve. I've had them hit the bait on the fall, so be sure to keep a tight line. Since catfish rely more on other senses than eyesight, I will use as heavy line as I can, and still be able to feel and work the bait well. Usually, ten or twelve pound monofilament during the day, and twenty-five pound braided line at night does the job. Plus, the greater breaking strength of the braided line helps me lose a few less lures to the bottom. Heavy monofilament deadens the action of the plug and the greater diameter lessens the depth the lure will run, so stick with braid at night.

Another place this technique will net you some fish is right below a riffle if the hole itself has plenty of cover and depth to hold shovelheads. Complex riffle/hole/riffles that include a bend or "S" curve in the river or where the riffle pours around both sides of an island are almost always much better than simple riffles. Expect the fish to be either in the run right below the riffle, or just below the dam, cruising any shallow rock bars for smaller fish late at night. One of my better spots I discovered after catching a 12-inch smallmouth that had a large injury scar around his midsection, where it apparently had narrowly escaped death from a big cat in the past.

Big cats are often shallow, and since they can feel any vibration, it pays to be stealthy and not stomp up and down the bank knocking over rocks. For this reason, and for safety sake, learn a spot thoroughly during the day before attempting to fish it at night. Also, turn away from the water when switching on a light to tie on a new lure. In spring, and again in fall when the water cools, shovelhead will feed actively during the day, and you can catch just as many fish in daylight. But still, in the heat of summer, nighttime is the right time for this action.

The beauty of this fishing is its simplicity. All you need are a half dozen lipless crankbaits, a rod and reel with some backbone, a good drag and nerves of steel.

THE LESSON

I'll call it Buford Creek. Its real name is something completely different. It is one of my favorite places in the world, and I try not to let everyone know where it is. It makes me nervous enough it's right there on the map, all ready for everyone to see. Anyway it's not really the creek itself that's the hotspot. Rather, it's what the creek does where it empties into the Little Miami River that creates the semi-secret spot. From what I can gather, around 14,000 years ago the last Ice age ended in Ohio. Huge torrents of meltwater cut the steep valleys of the Little Miami. This melting ice also created Buford Creek. So nowadays Buford Creek is a steep narrow gorge that really dumps a deluge into the LMR during violent storms. In quiet weather the creek is just about dry. Along with a flood of water Buford Creek also dumps hundreds of tons of rocks over the decades into the Little Miami, creating a big rock bar and riffle and pushing a bend into the Little Miami. This bend causes the river to cut into the far bank and forming a nice deep run and hole. To get to this spot you park out on the road that parallels the river and walk down the dry or at least almost so bed of Buford Creek to get to the river.

It's here in this last bit of creek just before it empties into the river, that years ago I had an epiphany that forever changed the way I fished. I was young then, and dumb, even though I thought I knew everything. By then, I'd learned that if I circled enough farm ponds throwing a quarter ounce spinnerbait I could catch a lot of largemouth bass, and I thought I was quite the fisherman. Well it was midsummer and hot. Too hot to try the farm ponds I'd been fishing during the day at least. So mostly to kill some time till evening I decided to fish the mouth of Buford Creek. I was walking down the creek, carrying my new shiny Shimano rod with the cardinal reel held in place with electrical tape, just like the pros in Bassmaster did. Then and there in front of me, I could see a minnow above the water of a tiny pool. From my vantage point it looked to be hovering a few inches above the water flopping its tail feebly. I crept closer and then sat down to watch.

From my new, closer look, I could tell it was a rather large minnow, held aloft by a rather small snake. When the snake held the minnow aloft he held the advantage but every time he lowered the minnow it would pull the little snake frantically around in a circle as the snake spun to keep its grip. Slowly the minnow weakened till the snake coiled around it and worked the minnow down its mouth.

As I sat there I could see something else flash in the pool. The water was so clear it was hard to tell where the edge of the tiny pool was. There in the pool was another minnow. I'm not sure if it was injured by the snake or just succumbing to the heat and the stress, but it was having a bad time . It would slowly swim along upright then list over to one side and slowly rise up towards the surface slowly beating its tail. Then the poor guy would struggle back down but only for a foot or two till it would stop, exhausted and then would slowly float back up only to repeat the whole thing again, in a slow dance of death. I had just read "Homer Circle" in Field and Stream and was struck by just how much the dying minnow looked like Homer's description of how to fish what he called a slim minnow plug.

Finally feeling like I was ready to succumb to the heat myself, I headed to the river. I knelt beside the dying fish and slipped my hat underneath and then raised it catching the helpless minnow in a cap full of water. I quickly walked the ten yards down to the river and waded in to mid-thigh depth. I lowered my hat into the water and freed the hapless minnow. It floated almost lifeless on the water's surface slowly working its fins as it floated downstream into the heart of the hole. When it was roughly fifteen feet away it beat its tail a few times diving weakly before floating back up. In the clear water I could see it coming, a big smallmouth, bigger than any I'd ever seen up till that time. It coasted up under the minnow and hung there. The minnow struggled weakly. Then the bass flared its gills and the minnow just disappeared.

I waded as quietly as I could back to shore and searched through my tackle box. It was a flat-sided Plano tackle box, one of the first I'd seen, and I was awfully proud of it. The box was stuffed full of things I'd bought and had been given to me by my dad.

Mostly largemouth lures like big plastic worms and buzzbaits. There in a crowded compartment along with two big crazy crawlers was a little gold and black Rapala dad had given me. It was too small to fish with the bait casting rod I'd been throwing spinnerbaits with, and I'd never used it. But this new spinning rod would throw it. I tied on the Rapala and began covering the pool with it. Fast. Too fast, just covering water like I had with my spinnerbaits. I began to sweat. I stopped, wiping the sweat out of my eyes as the Rapala floated out there. I guess in the perfect story this is where a bass would of nailed it. Instead it floated back over some sunken brush. I slowly pulled the lure back trying not to get it to swim too deep.

That's when the light bulb went off. I'd been hit over the head with it, first by Homer Circle and then given a demo by the dying minnow. But like I said, I was young and knew everything. The next cast I let the minnow sit there a minute, then twitched it and then reeled a bit; then let it float back up, and twitched it again.

After four or five feet of this a smallmouth of about a pound exploded on my Rapala.

And as they say, the rest is history. All through the bend pool and the run below, a dozen smallmouth fell victim to the little floating Rapala. Recently, while poking around my bookshelf looking for something to read, I found Homer Circle's old book, Bass Wisdom and the memory of that day all those years ago came rushing back. It's funny how you can forget where you left the car keys this morning, but remember every detail of a fishing trip thirty years before.

Many, like the emerald shiner, are found in open water and stay near the surface. They have no preference for a particular type of substrate. Along with gizzard shad, they are the main food of hybrid striped bass and their cousins, the white bass in the lower reaches of the Little Miami. Shiners are taller than they are thick, and are almost perfectly imitated by floating minnow plugs. Most shiner species are a pearl color, tinted with light shades of pink or green. Another good shiner imitation is a swim bait or shad body, three or four inches long.

Creek chubs are often the top predator in many of the smaller tributaries of the Little Miami River. They can reach almost a foot in length and feed on small invertebrates such as aquatic and terrestrial insect larvae. The biggest chubs can even take small crayfish. Creek chubs are a bit fatter in cross section than shiners and might be better imitated with a four inch grub or a fatter shad bait. Many creek chubs have a dark stripe that runs down their side. I sometimes doctor up pearl shad with waterproof markers from the craft store, adding a stripe or dash of color to them.

Bluntnose minnows, central stonerollers, and similar minnows are the most common small fish in the Little Miami over its entire length. Bluntnose minnows spawn over and over starting in spring through late summer. They spawn under logs, in brush or under rocks in shallow water. Females lay sticky adhesive eggs on the underside of whatever structure they spawn under. Stonerollers spawn just upstream or downstream of riffles in spring. Most minnow species of this size feed on algae growing on rocks, logs and brush in the river. All this adds up to more reasons to throw around good structure and cover besides the fact they are good staging and holding areas for bass. Sinking and suspending minnow plugs in deep runs above and below riffles and floating minnow plugs and topwaters fished around structure imitate these minnows well. Most inline spinners are also imitating these minnows. These minnows are right there, behind my number one bait for the LMR, a three inch smoke metal flake grub on a roundball jighead. This, at least in my eyes, perfectly matches the general size, color, and overall impression of these ubiquitous baitfish. If you match the size of the jighead to the depth of the water and speed of the current so your jig is swimming just off the bottom around riffles, runs, and good structure in the river, it's hard not to catch fish

on a smoke metal flake grub in the LMR.

Darters, sculpins, and madtoms populate the riffles and runs of the Little Miami. Most of these guys run two to four inches in length and average around three inches. They are both darker and more colorful than the minnows that frequent the slower river. Some, like the rainbow darter, are as colorful as any aquarium fish you will ever see. But most are mottled and camouflaged to blend with their surroundings. While minnows such as the stoneroller might be more common over the entire river, in certain riffles the majority of small fish will be darter species. These, along with hellgrammites and crayfish that frequent riffles, also make the shallow rocky riffles and runs of the LMR a dinner table for the river's bass.

There are eleven or twelve darter species in the LMR, with several being found together on most riffles. For this reason you may want to experiment with color choices. I like to throw things with just a touch of red or orange, as even some plainer darters show these colors when spawning. I'll usually throw a grub there that is darker than I throw in the slower waters of the river. This might be something like a motor oil metal flake or pumpkinseed. I also have a few grubs made by stringing a piece of orange living rubber with a large needle. I trim this to leave a short stubby piece sticking straight out of each side of the grub, right behind the jighead. These imitate the stiff pectoral fins of riffle minnows. Darters, sculpins and madtoms all use stiff side fins to help anchor themselves to bottom in the swift water of riffles. On many species these are red or orange in color. I also like to throw a small Rebel minnow as they are also good choices in fast water.

In summary, in the bends, holes and eddies of the river, I throw pearl, silvery, and chrome colored lures. Since shiners often feed and hold high in the water column these are also prime places to throw topwater plugs. I like lures with a flatter deeper profile here, like lipless cranks, shad bodies and flatter minnow plugs. Since shiners run a tad bigger, you can get away with a bigger lure here too. In swifter water such as riffles, runs, and chutes, I like a fatter rounder lure like a grub or a Rebel minnow, and a darker lure with a splash of color. A smaller lure, like a three inch grub or a marabou jig, is better here than a bigger one. That being said, there are no absolutes in this, just like any other kind of fishing. But at least I feel like I have a strategy and a place to start.

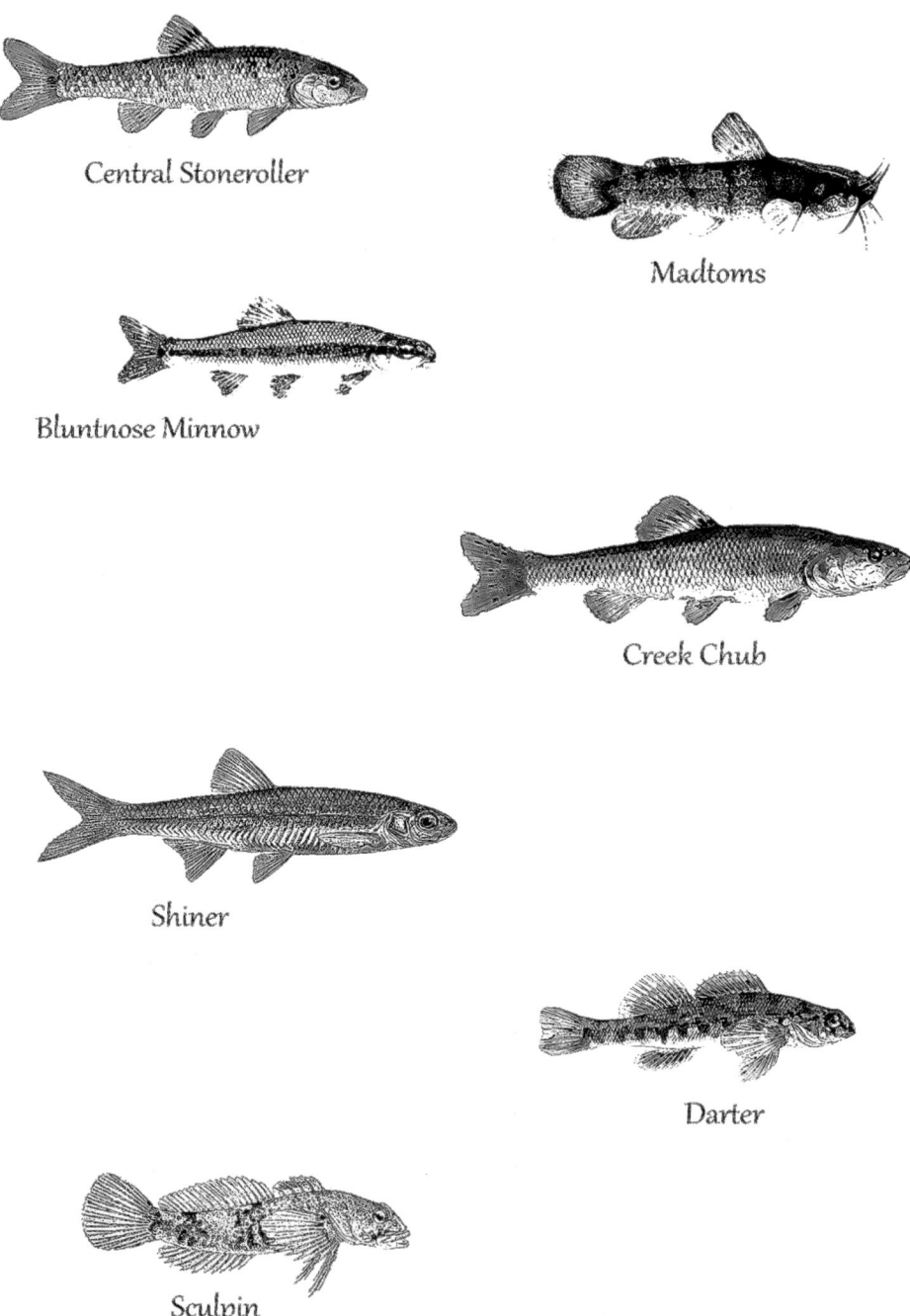

Common Minnows and Small Fishes of the LMR

Central Stoneroller

Madtoms

Bluntnose Minnow

Creek Chub

Shiner

Darter

Sculpin

Hellgie Fishing

What exactly is the hellgrammite? You hear everybody talking about them for smallmouth, but in my experience most fishermen have never seen one. Well, this guy is actually the flat multi-legged larva of the ferocious looking Dobsonfly. Both the larvae and the adults can pinch the heck outta you, so handle them with care. Actually it's only the female adults that really tend to hurt you.

Hellgrammites spend up to three years underwater in the larval form before crawling out on land to become a Dobsonfly. They only live about one week as an adult. The larvae live under rocks and leaves on the stream bottom where they are miniature monsters devouring smaller insects. I can't imagine the horror of being a little bug and having one of these monsters crawl over and grab me. I'm always a bit afraid of them when I seine one myself. But to the bass they are like French fries, just with lots of little legs and pincers.

When drifting hellgie nymphs with a fly rod, I use a floating fly line, long leader, weighted nymph, and strike indicators. I like the little pinch-on foam strike indicators for this. I'll set one indicator about a quarter of the length of the leader up from the leader butt and then another about halfway. Then as the fly tumbles into deeper water, I can first watch the one indicator then the other as the fly sinks. You want the fly tumbling along as deep as you can get it, preferably just ticking bottom every now and then. Set the hook on any pauses or jerks during your drift. Use a short cast, short as you can get away with without scaring the fish. It's a trade-off because longer casts won't scare fish but you miss most of your strikes by casting right over where the fish are lying. Cast upstream and across in the run right below a riffle. With only twenty feet or less of line out, you can follow the line by lifting the rod to keep as much slack out of the line as possible without dragging the fly as it sweeps down and past you.

I'll use twist-ons to get the fly down near the bottom, if I have to. Twist-ons are little lead strips packaged in little cardboard books like matches. They make casting awful, but you're only casting a few feet. In really swift water it can become the old chuck and duck. I generally tie my own hellgie flies, just generic black wooley buggers but with something like Swiss straw tied along the back. Examples of better known flies that imitate a hellgie include the EZ Mite by Orvis, Woolly Bugger, Murray's Hellgrammite, Delaware River Hellgrammite, Bitch Creek bug, Michael Verduin's Mighty Mite Hellgrammite pattern, or Braided Stone Fly Crawler by Percy's flies (world's best prices on flies by the way) all in as big a size as you can throw on whatever rod you have.

Reading The Water

Here we have a drawing of a productive stretch of river. Water quickens as a hole shallows and pours over a riffle that deepens into a run before the river deepens further into another pool. Long slow pools in the Little Miami typically have soft bottoms that provide little food for either bass or catfish.

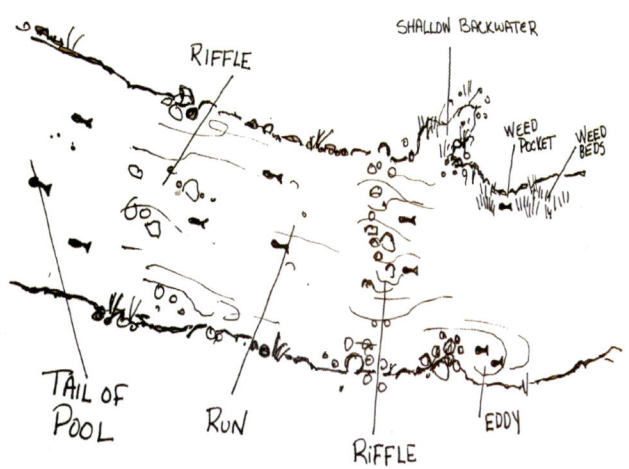

Often they run waist deep for hundreds of yards and when the water is clear you can see they are devoid of both cover and fish. But as the water speeds up at the tail of a pool, the bottom becomes hard, mostly a mixture of smaller gravel and rock, while the riffle/run below has bigger rocks mixed in. This area of hard bottom can run deceptively far up into the pool unseen from above the water, but where the bottom begins to harden it can hold fish. Often the faster water in the tail becomes smooth as it shallows and is known as a slick. In spring, after the water is sufficiently warm enough for smallmouth to be active, and all through fall, the tails of pools are the most consistent fish-producing spots on the river. I usually start out with an inline spinner cast cross current and quartering upstream, fan casting my way across the tail. An inline spinner's blades will not turn correctly if cast directly upstream so be sure to cast both across stream and upstream. If the tail has a slick, a topwater twitched as it sweeps downstream can be exciting as can a deer hair bug fished with a fly rod. Be sure to throw a few casts up farther into the hole in case the current has swept away the muck farther up into the hole than it looks. The tail of a big pool is a place I will often stop and fish again when walking out at the end of a fishing trip as fish drop back out of a pool and begin to feed, replacing those you might have hooked earlier. Some of the best spots on the river, the destination spots, have distinct tail/riffle/run/pool transitions from one pool to the next. These spots are also the food factories in the river. Hellgrammites, caddisflies, snails, baitfish, and crayfish abound.

The run or head of the pool is preferred habitat for small mussels. If deep holes and pools are the living rooms and bedrooms of the stream bass's world, think of the riffle and run as his kitchen and dining room. The run or deep end of a riffle is also a good place to search for feeding sauger, white bass, and channel cats. The water depth and speed can vary greatly over the length of a riffle/run and you can end up throwing half the lures in your box in one fifty-yard stretch. Don't be afraid to keep switching lures here as conditions dictate. Our drawing also shows a shallow backwater. These are often small fry nurseries and are filled with tiny fish seeking safety in the shallows. Late in the day or at first light can find bass patrolling the deeper edges of these backwaters. Deeper backwaters can also be a fun place to throw a dry fly for long-eared sunfish and other pan fish. At the bottom of runs, weed beds often begin; holes or breaks in these can hold bass, but they are mostly one fish spots. In the drawing below we see a smaller stream entering the main river flow. In flood these streams spew rocks out into the river and create their own rock bar and/or riffle

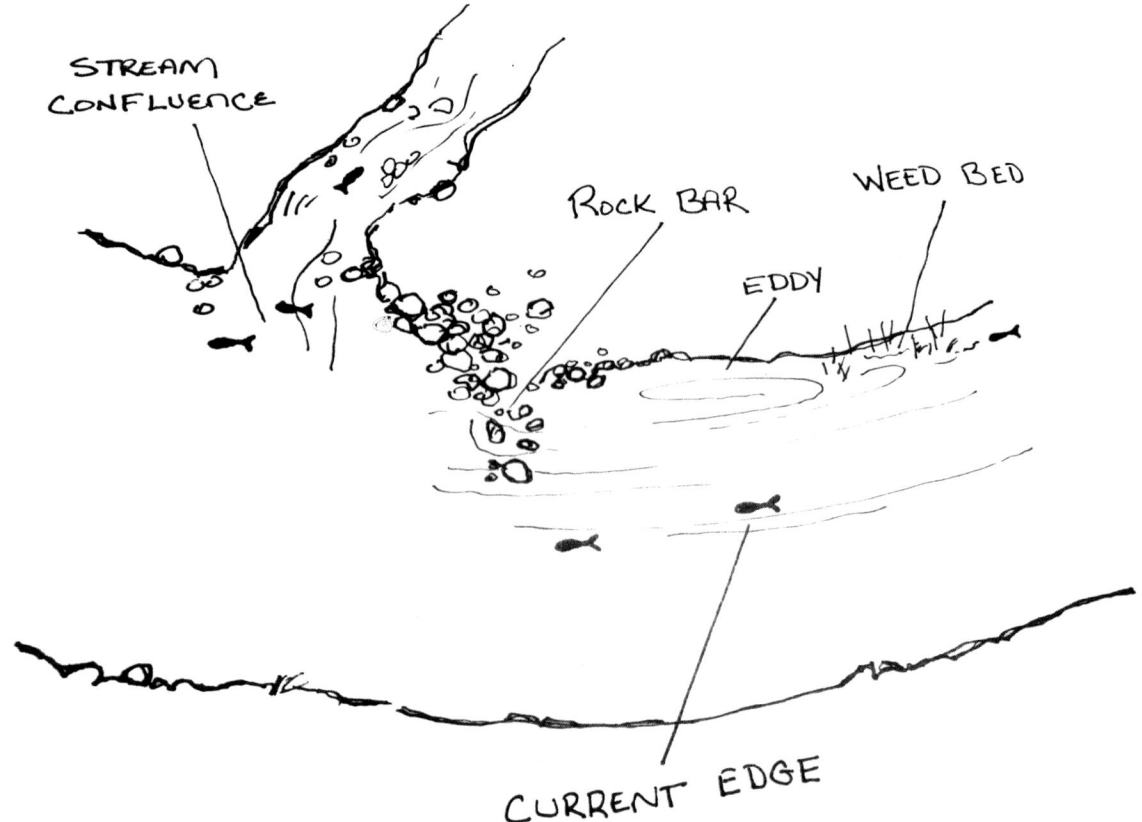

STREAM CONFLUENCE

ROCK BAR

WEED BED

EDDY

CURRENT EDGE

in the Little Miami. These act just like the riffles between the pools in the river, speeding up the water flow and creating a hard bottom and another food factory. These are great places to throw a grub or jig, letting it sweep downstream in the current off the end of the bar and into the bar's eddy. The water above the bar becomes like a miniature tail not unlike the tail of a pool and should be fished accordingly. As the water sweeps around the rock bar at the incoming creeks mouth it often creates a seam where fast water flows past slow water. This seam can extend for quite a ways downstream, holding fish. Here a fish can hold in slower water and dart out and catch food as it passes by. Here you also often see gar holding in clear water.

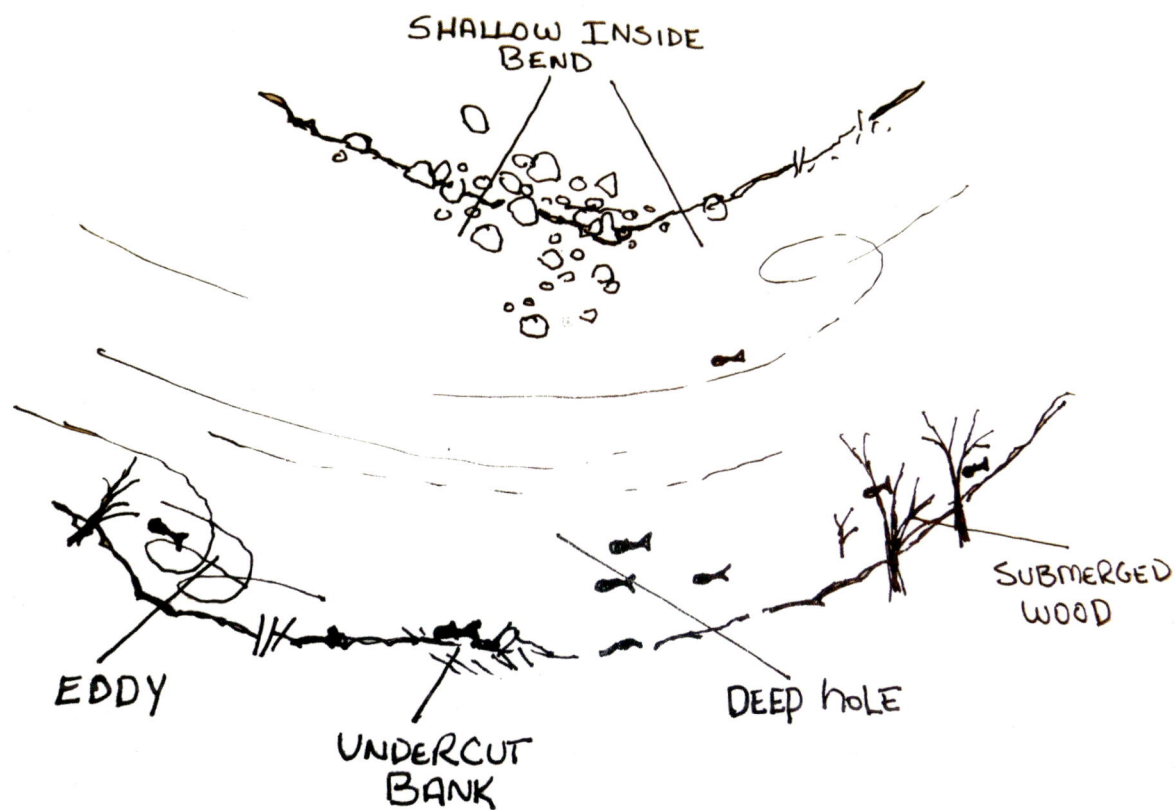

In the third picture (above) we have a bend in the river. Usually you can only fish such places from the shallow inside of the bend with the far bank being too steep to fish from. Very early and late in the day you can sometimes find bass herding minnows up on the shallow gravel of inside bends. If you cast ahead of these swirls with a small Rapala or inline spinner you almost always are rewarded with a jolting strike. The outside of river bends are typically the deepest spots in the river, as the current hits there full force in flood, scouring out a hole. If there is any flooded timber in the hole, here is where you want to try and catch that big shovelhead. The now defunct railroad often dumped huge amounts of stone and rip-rap along outside bends to control erosion. Here, with both current and cover, bass and catfish find good hunting, so the fishing's often great.

The best example of this kind of cover is the "Big Rocks" just upstream from South Lebanon. These kinds of spots, like distinct riffles/runs, are destination spots you plan a fishing trip around. A plastic grub might just be the best lure choice here but plan on losing a bunch of them to the rocks. Of course there are many other kinds of fish-holding spots in the river besides the ones listed above, bridge abutments, holes or cover in a pool etc., but they all usually have one thing in common, except in winter, when they congregate in deep pools. Gamefish in the river prefer rock or gravel to a mucky bottom. Find those rocky bottoms, with some moderately deep water nearby, and odds are you will find fish.

Taking the River's Temperature

Possibly the most important thing you can carry to the Little Miami is a thermometer. If you use it, that is. And not just one time, what's the river doing today, kind of thing. Though that's a good idea, take it a step further.

I'm by the mouth of O'Bannon Creek a lot. I've taken the temperature there a lot, and I've learned a lot. Often the river temperature will vary by three or four degrees from the creek. And the creek will affect the river for a long way downstream. It might take the river seventy-five yards to completely absorb the temperature impact on the river of a tributary like O'Bannon Creek. And every tributary has impact, some more than others.

The big ones, like Todd's Fork or Caesar's Creek or East Fork, have a lasting impact on the Little Miami main stem. These tributaries also make a huge difference some days in the clarity of the river. If it hasn't rained upstream, but we have a big thunderstorm locally, you can stand at the mouth of a creek like Turtle Creek, and see a band of brown muddy water extending way downstream. This helps me visualize the band of cooler or warmer water made by the tributary at other times too, where there is not a corresponding color change. On sunny days it's possible to feel a big temperature difference as you wade out of the shallower backwaters into the current of the main river. These shallow backwaters are like a car with the windows rolled up in the sun trapping heat, then releasing the super warm water into the main stem.

The Little Miami, especially in the headwaters, gets a percentage of its water from springs. This too has an effect on the temperature of the river. In winter, pools that have springs in them can draw bass like a magnet, because spring water can be warmer than water in the main stem that has been impacted by super cold air temperatures. Likewise areas where spring water enters the river can draw bass in the heat of the summer too, because the water is cool of about where the fish may be.

Below is a general guide to temperature and smallmouth behavior:

45 degrees and below- bass are very inactive. You might find one willing to take something like a hair jig under a float, but you're more likely not to.

46 to 50 degrees- Bass become slightly more active and more likely to strike a lure.

50 to 55 degrees- Smallmouth begin to move out of their wintering holes and move towards spawning areas. Look for them at staging areas along this route. Rocks, deep pockets out of the current are good places to try.

55 to 58 degrees- Bass begin to gather close to and on spawning areas. Often they will readily bite now.

58 to 64 degrees- Smallmouth are on the spawning grounds nesting.

65 to 70 degrees- Post spawn.

70 degrees and above- Bass move into their summertime haunts and become relative homebodies for the summer and early fall season using mainly just one pool and adjoining riffles.

65 degrees and cooler in fall- Bass begin to move back towards their wintering grounds and feed heavily till water cools below 50 degrees. Feeding is really pronounced from 61 to 56 degrees. This is the best big bass time of the entire year.

Night Time is the Right Time

Once the bass are finished with their post-spawn funk and water has settled into its summertime flow, it's pretty easy to catch at least some smallmouth in the LMR. Water temperatures are high; bass metabolism is high and they are constantly eating. Hit a riffle or run and throw a Rebel craw or an in line spinner and you will catch some fish. Just one problem though, they are likely to be small or medium sized fish.

So where do those big ones you were nailing last fall spend their summers? Actually you are probably fishing the right spot just at the wrong time. I catch dozens of bass every year with scars from near death experiences. Patches where a big shovelhead has grabbed one, funny bumps and bulges where something toothy like a saugeye or a mink has chomped on them when they were little. Fish with big holes poked in them by a great blue heron. Face it. It ain't easy being a fish. And fish don't get big doing dumb things. The biggest fish in the river have learned the safest time to be out prowling around or food is after dark. Once they get too big to be an easy meal for a big shovelhead, it's relatively safe for a big smallmouth to prowl around at night. Now, he's big enough to become one of those terrors stalking the night for smaller fish.

Riffles and runs are usually the best spots for locating active smallmouth during the summer. Food such as minnows, crayfish, and insects are plentiful in these areas and dissolved oxygen is higher. So bass love these places in summer. Even during the heat of the day on the hottest days, you can catch smallmouth on the riffles, you just don't catch the big ones. Bigger bass can catch bigger food and even though his metabolism is ramped up, a bigger fish can fill up on enough minnows and crayfish during low light to last during the heat of the day. So during the day, a big bass is backed up into a treetop, in a big bend, up under an undercut bank, or tight to a big rock in a deep hole. If you make a great presentation you might get him to strike, but that's not easy. Try coming back at night to those same spots you're catching small to medium-size bass during

the day, but pick a place you are very familiar with. Only a fool would mess around on an unfamiliar stretch of river at night.

Besides riffles, if you find a good hole with lots of structure or a big rock bar in a good bend, give those a try too. A topwater plug fished in the calm water of a pool in the middle of the night can draw big bass like a magnet. Simplicity is the name of the game when fishing at night. I'll often bring just a half-dozen lures I can carry in my pocket. It seems to me if a smallie is going to hit at night I can catch him on any reasonable lure choice. Usually you won't have to experiment around and fool the fish like you sometimes have to during the day. I wear a headlamp and bring an extra flashlight with me. If your batteries go dead, or something happens to damage your light, the last thing you want is to be out there in the dark without a spare. A great choice for night fishing is a lipless crankbait. A big one, say

a half-ounce or three quarter ounce model works best. This is often all I'll throw if I'm fishing a big bend pool. Big smallmouth, shovelheads, and saugeye will move up shallow on the rock bar to feed at night and you can catch all three on a lipless. I must have caught at least two dozen shovelhead last year on the Little and Great Miami rivers, fishing a lipless crankbait at night. And I also caught two saugeye that qualified for the Fish Ohio awards program, as well as some of the nicest bass of the year. During the summer, bass are homebodies, and if you tangle with a big smallie during the day and lose him, you can fish that area during the night and up your chances of hooking him again. Just like during the day, the better the spot you fish at night the better your fishing will be. And since I'm not going to be as mobile as I would be during the day, it becomes important to pick a good spot to try at night, with good and easy access.

Alone Time

I like myself best when I'm by myself.

Alone, poking around the river, I find the time to think about more than TV, politics, cell phones, text messages, taxes and other unwholesome topics. Alone, sometimes I'll stop, sit on a rock, and just watch the river, something I'd never get around to if I were out fishing with someone else. Odd, but also true, I'm more likely to catch a bigger fish by myself too. I'll try something different, experiment.

Let's face it, a lot of big fish don't get caught because someone is just trying to catch just as many fish as the other guy. The few folks I do go fishing with seem to feel that same way on some level. They are about as likely as me to wander off into the bushes for an hour or two looking at inky cap mushrooms or fallen leaves. But these same folks are just as likely as me to fish too hard in driving rain or snow, because their gut tells them to. We sometimes end up back at the truck having fished the same stream for five or six hours having only spoken five or six words. But somehow we "went fishing together." Like me, they appreciate the value of alone time.

Sometimes when I am fishing by myself I bring a small sketch pad in my pack. Sometimes it sits there untouched, but occasionally it adds so much to my time spent outside. It forces me to slow down, notice things, and look at the things I miss most of the time. Could anything be better training for a fisherman? For being a person? Who knows, eventually if I draw enough I won't be such an old fuddy-duddie.

PART TWO

Way Upstream – Clifton Gorge Area

Above Clifton Gorge the Little Miami is what the Ohio Department of Natural Resources calls "a small meandering stream". But in the gorge everything changes. Pinched in between dolomite cliffs, the melt water of the retreating glaciers cut straight down and in cascades and deep whirlpools, a river was born. Walk the trail that follows the gorge in wet weather, and waterfalls from the many springs and seeps cascade over the cliffs into the river below.

LMC Photo courtesy of Ronald G. Levi

Due to the fact it's reasonably flat right until you step off into space it's almost impossible to convey in a photograph the scale of the gorge. All the photos I've seen do no better than my poor attempts. Trust me, this is one place a hundred times more impressive in person than any picture can show. In this stretch, the normally knee to waist deep upper Little Miami River rages along between the cliff walls at a depth of 34 feet!

Darnell's leap: In January 1778, the Shawnees captured Daniel Boone and his party of 28. Cornelius

Darnell was able to flee, and with Shawnee in hot pursuit, Darnell leapt across the twenty-five-foot gap between the cliffs to freedom. Of course, he could not make the entire leap. But branches hung out over the 80 foot drop and Darnell went crashing across into them, finally grabbing one as he fell and climbing up the cliff to safety! It makes me uneasy here to lean out over the safe rail of the overlook. I cannot begin to imagine the courage it took to attempt the leap. In fact there have been dozens of tragic deaths in the gorge over the years. One of the earliest stories is that of a woman and child abducted by Shawnee Indians. As her husband struggled with one of the Shawnee both men slipped off the cliff, never to be seen again. Even now someone is killed every few years by falling from the cliffs or drowning in the swift waters of the gorge.

Famous Steamboat Rock (below), so named because, well, it looks like a big steamboat floating midstream.

The river here drops at a powerful rate of 35 feet per mile. Just downstream in John Bryan State Park, the rock is slightly softer, and the gorge opens to a quarter mile or so wide, but still retains impressive cliffs.

Below Clifton Gorge State Nature Preserve, the trails enter John Bryan State Park. The two parks are really separated only by name and management strategy, as they fit seamlessly together and you cannot tell walking the river when you cross the boundary.

In 1896 John Bryan purchased 335 acres along the Clifton Gorge area, and called these acres "Riverside Farm." The Cincinnati-Pittsburgh stagecoach road served the area, and settlers started up water-powered industries, such as a textile mill, gristmills, and sawmills, in the gorge. After the turn of the century, water power was no longer as economical for electricity, and the industries in the rugged gorge

closed. At the top of the gorge is the town of Clifton with one of the two surviving mills along the Little Miami. Clifton Mill is known for its Christmas light display and restuarant.

John Bryan gave Riverside Farm to the state of Ohio in 1918, "to be cultivated by the state as a forestry, botanic and wildlife reserve park and experiment station," which would bear his name. John Bryan State Park and Clifton Gorge State Nature Preserve have been designated as a National Natural Landmark by the U.S. Department of the Interior.

The best base for exploring these upper reaches of the river has to be the town of Yellow Springs. Located just a few miles from John Bryan and Clifton Gorge, Yellow Springs is named after the huge spring that adds its water through beautiful Glen Helen Nature Preserve to the river. The spring gets its name from the rocks of the spring colored by the minerals in the water. Supposedly the waters of the spring cure all that ails you, and spas and resorts were built nearby in the early 1900s. Long before that, however, Robert Owen founded the village in 1825. Robert Owen wanted to build a commune where everyone would work together for the common good. His idea seems to have worked better in theory than in practice, as a year later the experiment broke up.

The town today has one of the quaintest little downtowns you will ever see. There are dozens of small shops offering everything from psychic readings, to handmade pottery, tie dye shirts, used books, Buddha statues or parkas made out of alpaca wool. A large portion of the tiny town's population seems to be connected to the sixties culture of college students from Antioch College and other Ohio schools whose students were known to espouse liberal causes at the time. Today, one might still find an occasional old car with bumper stickers stating "save the whales" or "make love not war." Yellow Springs is the best place I know to buy that one-of-a-kind gift you know no one else has ever seen, much less bought. There are some very nice jewelery stores, craft shops, bike shops, quality restaurants, as well as bed and breakfasts to accommodate a lively tourist trade. There is also a quaint little tavern downtown that might just serve the perfect steak fries.

Adding to Yellow Springs' charm are the legends surrounding Glen Helen. The beautiful valley, according to local lore, was a sort of lover's lane for the Shawnee. Supposedly visitors have seen a ghostly Indian maiden, or heard her call for her long lost love. Glen Helen is a 1000-acre nature preserve affiliated with the newly re-opened Antioch College. Filled with cliffs, interesting rock formations, and the famous spring, the preserve is on my must-see list for anyone in the upper watershed.

Tecumseh Preserve

Downstream a few miles from Yellow Springs, just north of Xenia at a place called Old Town is the Tecumseh Preserve, owned by the Little Miami Conservancy (FKA Little Miami Inc.) This 82 acre preserve is located on the site of Chalahgawth, the Shawnee capital and boyhood home of the great Shawnee leader, Tecumseh. Even when he was a young boy, the Shawnee sensed greatness in Tecumseh. Possibly because of this, in the winter of 1776 Tecumseh's father, the great warrior Black Fish, summoned him and told him it was time to seek his Pa-wah-ka. A Pa-wah-ka was regarded as a magical object through which one could talk to and receive power from the Great Spirit. Black Fish told Tecumseh he must strip every day and run naked to the nearby Little Miami River, and plunge into the river before returning home. Well this went on day after day. Through snow or cold sleet and rain he ran to plunge into the Little Miami.

As winter wore on Tecumseh would have to break through the ice formed on the river's edge. All this barefoot and naked mind you. What a test of sheer willpower this must have been for Tecumseh. Finally in mid-January, Black Fish told Tecumseh that the next run would be his last, that Tecumseh was to wade to the middle of the river and dive to the bottom, and close his hands on whatever he touched and bring that back to Black Fish without looking at it. Tecumseh ran naked to the river, plunged in and returned with a small white quartz rock. Black Fish declared this his Pa-wah-ka, and Tecumseh forever afterward wore it on a string around his neck. I imagine it must have been priceless to him considering what he endured to earn it.

At the dedication ceremony for the preserve held October 5, 2013, Tecumseh returning to his home was portrayed by Ross Shaw. I took this photo (below) of him fording the Little Miami in that ceremony. Credit for this nice preserve should be given to the Little Miami Conservancy, the Tecumseh Land Trust, The Upper River Fund, Ohio EPA, and the Greene County Commissioners. Their combined resources, together with some grant money and months of negotiation resulted in the preservation of this historic place, protected in its natural state for posterity. There have been numerous success stories just like this one involving preservation and reclamation of land along the Little Miami River. While these may sometimes seem to just spring up, they are really the result of hard work by caring folks dedicated to the preservation of this special river.

Since 1967, the Little Miami Conservancy has acquired land in the Little Miami River Watershed, creating over 100 nature preserves along the Little Miami River. Like many of them, the Tecumseh Preserve is a conservation site dedicated to preservation and restoration of the wetlands, wooded river corridor, and the return of the site to its natural state as it was 250 years ago.

The "return to nature" strategy is not so much for sentimental reasons, but more to conserve and protect this outstanding river ecosystem by restoring the wetlands, trees and grasses along the river that filter runoff, and preserve water quality and fish and wildlife habitat. To this end, at the Tecumseh Preserve, the Little Miami Conservancy has already planted 45 acres of native prairie grasses and more than 10,000 trees (mostly oaks) along the river corridor.

The Tecumseh Preserve is not a recreational site generally open to the public, but more of a restoration project. Access to the site may be arranged by appointment by contacting the Little Miami Conservancy.

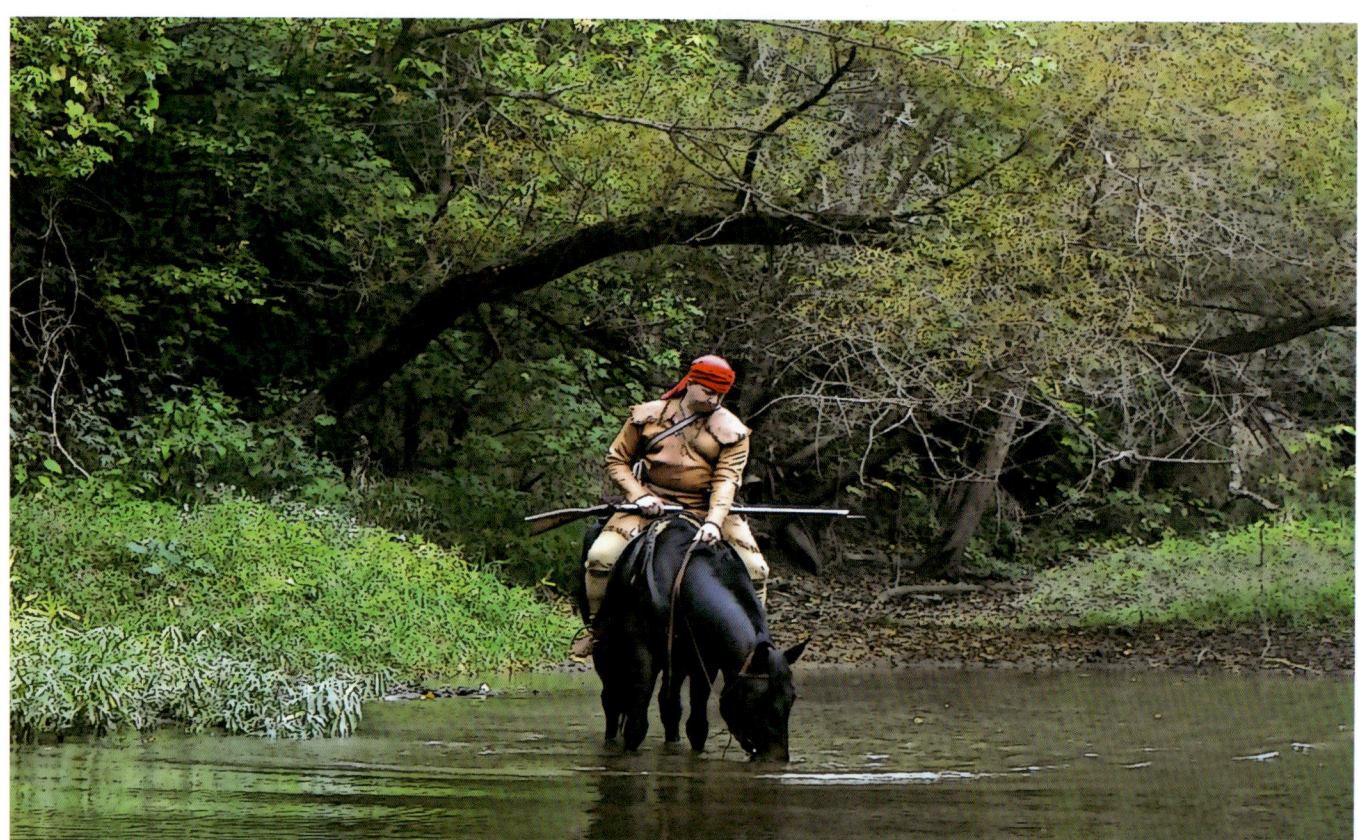

ROSS SHAW PORTRAYING TECUMSEH RETURNING TO HIS BOYHOOD HOME ALONG THE LITTLE MIAMI

This section of the LMR, a mile upstream of the Tecumseh Preserve, is a nice mixture of pools and riffles with lots of fallen trees. A fun wade on a hot summer day, I've never caught a big smallie here, but the chance to fish with the ghosts of the past more than makes up for that.

The Narrows

Located in Greene County, The Narrows Preserve is one of my favorite spots anywhere. There the glacier pushed the river out of its bed and the river cut this valley forming a new one.

Formerly owned by the Iddings Family, The Narrows is a long skinny park with a wide level trail that offers excellent access to the Little Miami River. Just above the park, the river twists and turns away from the road and offers some great fishing to anyone willing to bushwhack. Downstream in the park there are some of the finest trees you will ever see, with huge sycamores, hundreds of years, old lining the river. About a half mile downstream of the parking lot, two huge trees, one on each side of the river, are strong candidates to be the biggest in the whole watershed.

The lower half of the park is a great place early and late in the day to spot wildlife such as deer, although on nice evenings the trail often populates with hikers. The big trees draw pileated woodpeckers, and the park is a bird watchers delight. Early one spring, I heard rustling leaves and stepped off the trail along this lower stretch to investigate, finding a half dozen garter snakes just out from hibernation. One of the best looks I've ever had of a mink was also in the Narrows. The mink foraged along the riverbank, coming within ten feet of me before realizing I was

an awfully funny looking tree, and bounded off. There is quite a bit of beaver sign in the park's lower half. Walking the trail quietly and watching the river right after daylight is a good way to spot these giant rodents.

I've also been startled by beaver slapping their tails in alarm when they spotted me first. At about a mile and a quarter from the trailhead the river turns, creating a long riffle/run/riffle called Brenda's Riffle that offers some of the best fishing in the river's upper half. A lovely creek enters the river there too, and a primitive campsite (permit only) located nearby is a great base camp to spend a long weekend exploring the river and surrounding woods.

The Snake-Roxanna and Spring Valley

So you've walked all the way down to Fishpot Ford, bushwhacked back up to the truck, then a week or two later maybe you found the old King's dam in the thickets below the old junction. You might even have sniffed out a riffle or a hole or two that it seems like only you know about. You're starting to think you know the river about as well as anybody.

But there are those pesky rumors. Your buddy that can't fish a lick, but is one of those hard core macho kayaker dudes, tells you about the place where the river bent hard back on itself, then back the other way again, and again till he wasn't quite sure which way was east or west anymore. You ask where, and he seems vague, mutters something about no roads and strainers and changes the subject. Six months go by and you overhear some guy's nightmare canoe story, how they ended up coming out after dark, and how the river twisted and turned just like in the kayaker's story. There's no place like that on the Little Miami, right? Idly, you ask where he took out and later with a little help from Google maps you're looking at this twisted rope of blue. Welcome to "The Snake."

So how do you get there? It sits a mile above the road at Spring Valley Wildlife Area's unknown little access ramp. Right behind that old gravel pit, you know the one, with so many no trespassing signs you're not sure if they would have you arrested if they caught you cutting through, or just shoot you. That one. There are a lot of fish there, though. And if you like the fly rod, bring it. Although the river's a third of its size down at Foster, all those rock bars give you room to back cast and the river's full of strainers and stumps that hold rock bass. The smal-

lies don't cooperate, but willingly bop a fly.

This is another section of the river where the existence of a quality canoe livery, with a full line of rental boats and livery services, opens up a really great section of the river that would otherwise be pretty hard to access. For many years, RiversEdge Outfitters, located about five miles up State Route 42 from Waynesville, has provided such services. They offer three main trips but are open to your own tailor-made outing. Each of their three offerings begins with a shuttle to a launch place upstream of their livery, and ends back at the livery. The shortest one is about a 2 ½ to three-hour paddle. The longest is about six hours. Those times do not account for beaching your boat to fly cast or spin fish along the way. There is another trip that can start from Rivers Edge that is unadvertised, and might take a little persuasion to get them to provide. I have not done this myself but I have heard from others it is a very fun and worthwhile trip for those with some paddling experience and willingness to make one serious portage around the Corwin Dam.

Remember Corwin dam, back down by Waynesville? Well, from RiversEdge, you can start at the livery and paddle downstream toward Waynesville through a wonderful stretch of river that hardly anyone ever fishes or paddles. Why? Because as you paddle down there you approach the Corwin Dam from the upstream side, and have to portage river left, around the dam to continue down the last mile to the Clint Fultz public access at Corwin. The up-side of this is you get to paddle and fish a great stretch of river, hardly ever used by anyone, and you have access to the great fishing below Corwin Dam, before taking out about half a mile further downstream.

However you manage to get in, (canoe, parachute maybe?) bring bug spray, lunch (it's gonna take a while), and wear jeans to try and protect yourself from the nettle jungle. Or better yet, take my advice when I say the fish are bigger downstream, the wading's easier, the access is easier, and just put the snake on that list of places you're going to fish "someday" and leave it to us crazy people for now.

Downstream of the snake, the river flows through the Spring Valley Wildlife Area. There's a nice little access road that seems known only to the dove hunters that hit the sunflower fields in the fall. Between the sunflower fields and the river sits a classic river bottom that has some majestic trees. You can find big Sycamores scattered all up and down the length of the river but there is a grove of real giants there.

Further downstream the river flows by the marsh in Spring Valley Wildlife Area, one of the best bird watching spots in the state if not the whole eastern US. More than 230 species have been seen here. Yep, that's not a typo, 230; a lot of states haven't even listed that many in the whole state. The marsh also holds beaver, otters, deer, muskrats galore, and decent fishing for panfish and largemouth bass. There's a nice trail around the marsh and a long boardwalk runs out into the cattails at the upper end. It's high on my list of places to critter-watch and just explore, with everything from bald cypress trees in the water to overgrown fields and upland woods. The river there has a few bass-holding riffles, some long pools, and lots of wood and trees in the water. I can usually count on having the water to myself and like to just kick back there and catch some channels and drum on nightcrawlers and enjoy the quiet.

Waynesville and Corwin

What's Waynesville and what's Corwin?

Well, Corwin was constructed to service the railroad as it crept up the Little Miami, so everything on the railroad side of the river is Corwin while the other side of the river is Waynesville. I'm going to do what everyone else does and make the people of Corwin mad by calling the area Waynesville. Waynesville slash Corwin may be one of the best bases to fish the Little Miami over its whole length. There is an abundance of parking, nice restrooms, restaurants with good food, and yes, great fishing.

Waynesville, now known for its excellent quality antique and craft shops, and famous for its annual Sauerkraut Festival in the fall, was historically a milling town. It still boasts the remains of the mill-race and the old mill dam, often now referred to as the Corwin Dam. Shown in the picture below, the Corwin Dam is an historic low head dam that was built from large stones without concrete.

While the dam backs up sediment from upstream, downstream of the dam, the oxygenated water attracts, smallmouth, saugeye, and other fish making it a good bet for casting into the white frothy water.

Below the Corwin Dam is another good spot to catch sauger and smallmouth bass, though in summer it's a popular swimming hole. Some mills operated there from 1800 until steam power ended the mill business. The millrace was then used as a swimming and picnic area in the 1930's and 40's under the names "Wayne Park" and "Old Mill Stream."

In 1952 L. D. Baker and Tom Norris opened a mill-race fishing concession. In the 1960's an old country store was added and in the 70's a swimming pool. More recently, until 2010, Der Dutchman restaurant and gift shop was located on the millrace until an unfortunate fire decimated the building and closed the restaurant. Just downstream from there, the river flows beneath route 73 and makes a couple sharp bends. A path leads from the scenic trail alongside 73 to the river, providing easy access. The bends have created several gravel bars and eddies that provide some interesting fishing. The gravel bars seem to change nearly every winter with high water, but almost always create some great fish-holding spots, sometimes in different locations nearby. Last time I was there the current had gouged out a deep hole over my head in depth, only two feet off the bank. I caught seven smallmouth without moving, on a marabou jig pitched into the deep hole underhanded.

Downstream the river slows and is lined with downed trees that hold plenty of catfish, panfish, and rock bass. Legend also has it that while his army was camped there during the Indian campaign in 1793, General "Mad" Anthony Wayne's paymaster hid the soldier's payroll somewhere along the river there during an attack by the Indians. The money has never been found! Something to think about when wading the river looking for a smallmouth. This area was well known to the first white explorers to contain a lot of wild game. In his wonderful book, *The Pioneer Writings of Josiah Morrow*, Dallas Bogan relates stories of bear hunting in 1797, stating that the early hunters found deer, bear, and wild turkey, plentiful in the area. Nowadays, history

is working to repeat itself, as deer and turkey are becoming common, and recently a bear was reportedly photographed nearby.

Fishing access to Corwin Dam can be difficult. The dam can be easily seen and reached by road, driving up the Corwin side about a mile then looking left toward the river. If you don't see the dam, roll down your car window and you will surely hear it. There, just below the dam, turbulence from the downstream side has gouged away and eroded the left descending bank close to the road. There, the dam can be seen without even getting out of the car. However, at this writing, the dam itself and adjoining banks on both sides of the river are privately owned, and there is no defined public access. For boaters, this is a required portage when approaching the dam from the upstream side. There is a portage path that passes through a wooded area just above the dam and passes within 20 feet of the road. Although the well-traveled portage path leads right to the nearby concrete dam abutment where kayaks and canoes are routinely portaged around the dam, it is still private property, and it cannot be assumed the landowner permits fishing access there.

A mile downstream, there is a public park on both sides of the river adjacent to the bridge that carries Corwin Avenue across the river connecting Corwin and Waynesville. On the Corwin side, the park is named Clint Fultz Memorial Park. It is a Warren County Park District park that features a public river access, parking and portable bathrooms. This is a great place to launch a canoe or kayak for a paddle or fishing trip from Corwin down to the public access at Middletown Road, or on to Oregonia or Mathers Mill public access just below Oregonia.

On the Waynesville side of the river, right across from Clint Fultz Park and Watercraft access at Corwin, the park is Bowman Park, also a Warren County Park facility, with public parking and portable toilets. Bowman Park also has nearly a half mile of frontage on the Waynesville side of the Little Miami River.

Waist Deep at Fishpot Ford

From the outside the stone is a riddle;
No one knows how to answer it.
Yet within, it must be cool and quiet
Even though a cow steps on it full weight,
Even though a child throws it in a river,
The stone sinks, slow, unperturbed
To the river bottom
Where fishes come to knock on it
And listen.

by Charles Simic

When I take the trip to fish the Ford, I usually park in the nature preserve lot at the mouth of Caesar Creek, and walk down the scenic trail. After about half a mile you pass the boundary of the Caesar Creek Nature Preserve, and the wide river bottom between the scenic trail and river becomes a huge cornfield. I keep walking downstream, even though a tractor path follows the preserve boundary down to the river and curves downstream to the ford. But the open gate has an old keep out sign that somehow seems more serious than most, and I keep walking. Another half mile walk and a shallow grass-covered drainage cuts across the cornfield straight to Fishpot. There at Fishpot Ford, the river is at its best. You are now deep into the really good water quality, and above the busiest of the canoe rentals. Luckily, the best fishing on the Little Miami is early morning and at dark.

About the time the canoes and kayaks show up there the fishing is pretty much done for the day anyway.

Fishpot Ford gets its name from John Sublett. Sublett was one of the earliest settlers and lived with the Rev. James Smith family at the mouth of Caesar Creek around 1798. There, he built chairs and furniture in a log workshop, but was best known as a hunter and fisherman. He excelled so much that he was famous as a hunter and fisherman, at a time when everyone was a hunter and a fisherman. At the head of the riffle complex at the ford John built a stone fish trap to catch the plentiful fish of the river. This stone trap stood many years, and gave the place its name.

The ford itself was well known long before John Sublett, though, as the main Indian trail from Old Chillicothe to the Ohio River crossed the Little Miami right there. General George Rogers Clark led his army across the river there in 1780, in his campaign against the Indian villages in Ohio. General Josiah Harmar also crossed there in 1790. Simon Kenton was a captain in that army, and Daniel Boone was a scout. There, the Little Miami splits in two then rejoins and splits again as the river makes two sharp turns. All this twisting and turning makes for several fish holding riffles, pockets, runs and eddies. I usually bring along a knapsack with a lunch, for if the fish are biting it's possible to spend half the day right there and never wade back upstream to the truck.

I usually bring along a varied lure selection, because of the varied water.

Fishpot Ford is roughly fifty miles upstream from the Ohio River and the water quality and diversity probably peaks through there. Close to 100 species of fish have been found in the Little Miami and a single rock in the river may be covered by a million algal cells, of at least a hundred species. An astounding eleven hundred plus species of algae and invertebrates make the Little Miami home. Twenty-three of these were new to science when discovered in the Little Miami River.

Just upstream from the ford is a nice hole full of downed trees and logjams. If I were trying to catch a big flathead from the river this is the first place I'd head. I'll often slip a container of chicken liver in my pack and after fishing the ford below with lures or flies, switch and catch channel cats there. The hole ends in a rock bar that's good for another smallmouth or two by using a weighted streamer fly or a grub fished on a jighead.

A little ways upstream, you re-enter the boundary of the nature preserve. From there to the mouth of Caesar Creek, the river makes two more sharp turns, and is good fishing all the way. Even if you plan on wading the entire way, wear jeans instead of shorts, as the river bottom vegetation is thick and filled with stinging nettles. In some places the river is simply not wadeable, so you have to climb out onto the bank and encounter the unfriendly vegetation. The preserve there is also overrun with whitetail deer. It's common to see a half dozen or so on every fishing trip.

John Sublett hunted deer, turkey, and bear all along there and once killed a black bear over four hundred pounds on the ridge overlooking the river. He also trapped fur-bearing animals such as beaver and otter, and is said to have trapped wolves on the ridge to the south. Beaver and otter have made a strong comeback in that section of the LMR. The river bottom there has lots of beaver sign and cuttings. At the mouth of Caesar Creek, a nice rock bar lines the bank, while weed beds extend to the mouth of the creek. In most flows, gar hang around the mouth and big carp can be seen slipping in and out of the creek. An in line spinner almost always produces a couple smallmouth, while nightcrawlers produce sheephead, carp, and catfish.

The short, final stretch of Caesar Creek from its mouth up to the parking lot at the State Nature Preserve is good fishing for smallmouth bass. The creek is beautiful, and a great place to bring a fly rod, as the creek is thigh deep and wide enough for a good back cast. There the Smith family tapped sugar maples in late winter, and the Reverend Smith drove a wagon-load of maple sugar and bacon from pigs, fattened on acorns, to market at Cincinnati a couple times a year. He slept in the wagon at the market where Fountain Square now stands before returning the next day.

Upstream 2 ½ miles from the State Nature Preserve parking lot, Caesar Creek flows down toward the Little Miami, as the tailwater from the Caesar Creek dam. This section travels through a deep gorge and has fair fishing for smallmouth bass in a beautiful setting. At one point large cliffs cut into the hillside, and beaver sign is common along the creek. Once I heard a loud ruckus while fishing and looked up just in time to see a large coyote leap off the bank trying to catch a goose standing on a small midstream island.

The Caesar Creek dam impounds 2800 acres of water up to one hundred ten feet deep forming the well-known Caesar Creek Reservoir. The first quarter-mile of tail water, right below the dam, holds a large variety of fish. I've caught largemouth, smallmouth, Kentucky spotted bass, sauger, pumpkinseeds, catfish, carp, sheephead and white bass there. Just last spring I lost a big muskie right below the dam. A few years ago, while carp fishing, I caught a five-foot-long paddlefish on light spinning tackle, then a month later landed another one four feet long. My best guess is that these filter feeders accidentally suck up the bait as they strain the water through huge gill slits. I don't pretend to know much at all about the reservoir even though I fish it a lot. The reservoir holds large numbers of crappie and sauger and is making a name for itself as a muskie lake. There is also an annual white bass spawning run, usually in May, when thousands of white bass come out of the reservoir heading up the upper section of Caesar Creek to spawn. A fisherman with a fly rod or light spinning tackle can enjoy amazing results when targeting these, sometimes catching 50 fish a day or more.

Tragedy and Beauty - A Tale of Two Bridges

In 1889 the Columbia Bridge Company of Dayton, Ohio was contracted to build a bridge across the Little Miami at Mather's Mill at a cost of $5,400. What followed is one of the saddest tales that ever took place along the river. As construction neared completion it began to rain. And it rained off and on for two weeks. Even though the river became swollen with high water the work went on unabated. A temporary trestle was built on which the completed span was to rest while the permanent supports were erected. Finally this was built and on Monday morning, January 20, 1890, the underpinnings of the bridge were being cut through and the bridge was being lowered to its final resting place on the new permanent supports. But just as the last few connections were being cut the high water swept away the temporary trestle and the bridge toppled into the river. William DeBord was pinned under the wreckage of the bridge with just his head above the icy January flood waters.

Several men held his head up for hours as workers struggled in vain to free him from the twisted iron

work of what remained of the bridge. It was reported that a Henry Breen held DeBord's head for at least three hours himself and several others took turns and the doomed man slowly succumbed to injury and hypothermia. I cannot imagine the mental scars these men must have carried with them for the rest of their days.

Today a new bridge stands in place of the old one and local legend has the place being haunted by DeBord's ghost. Just upstream now is a campground and campers have claimed to have heard his ghost moaning in the night. I cannot say if this is true,

but it seems if any place has a right to be haunted, it's here.

The best fishing I've found is to wade upstream of the impressive Corwin Nixon covered bridge, dedicated in 1982. Here the river splits pouring around a large island. At the top of this, in the riffle is built a make-shift dam of river stones. This dam has an opening about ten feet across that channels the current into the hole below. Here I've caught most of the different gamefish in the river. A small crankbait produces a smallmouth bass or two most trips. I've fished nightcrawlers here, throwing them out unweighted and letting the current wash them downstream. This has produced a channel or two, plus drum and several species of sucker.

Fort Ancient- Will o' Wisps & Warrior Ghosts

You are lost in the desolate forest
Where the stars give a pitiful light.
But the far-away glow of the Will of the Wisp
Offers hope in the menacing night.
It is lonely and cold in the forest,
And you shiver with fear in the damp,
As you follow the way of the Will of the Wisp
And the dance of it's flickering lamp.
But know, as you trudge through the forest,
Toward that glistening torch in the gloom,
That the eerie allure of the Will of the Wisp
Summons you down to your doom.
It will lead you astray in the forest,
Over ways never traveled before.
If ever you follow the Will of the Wisp,
You'll never be seen anymore.

By Jack Prelutsky

Few places along the Little Miami River offer more beauty, history, natural features, and recreational opportunities than the section known as Ft. Ancient. Aside from all that, at Ft. Ancient there is probably better fishing, and more ghosts along both banks than anywhere else. It is known that from the end of the last ice age a number of cultures have lived there, including Paleo-Indians, Adena, Hopewell,

Fort Ancient peoples, Woodland cultures and Scots-Irish pioneers. The hill overlooking the river is a site to visit if you are interested in Native American cultures in Ohio. Two and a half miles of earthworks, some up to twenty feet tall, Indian mounds, Indian burials, villages, farming and religious sites are all there. You name it, Fort Ancient has it all.

Down the floodplain, where now the well-known Morgan's Outdoor Center and canoe livery is located, was the site of a pioneer settlement, now completely gone. This ghost town had a blacksmith shop, hotel, post office, and was a stop on the Little Miami Railroad. On the opposite bank of the river the Cross Keys Tavern, built in 1802, still stands. The Cross Keys was also a stop on the stagecoach line. Local lore has the tavern was haunted by a woman who stayed there while the Cross Keys was operated as an inn, probably sometime around 1810. Supposedly she found her bed so comfortable that after she died she returned to haunt that bed. Legend also says the antique shop at the top of the hill has tried selling the bed but it keeps getting returned by unhappy buyers. The antique shop itself was originally a church built in the 1850's. I've heard the abandoned cemetery beside the shop is haunted itself. Across the road from the graveyard, in Camp Kern, is the Kern Effigy. A stone pathway built by the Hopewell supposedly resembles a giant snake, though I have a hard time seeing the snake.

My Dad, brother and my Great Uncle Albert Sandlin fished the river along there in the 1970's and saw their own ghost of sorts, a ball of light floating downriver hanging a few feet above the water. My Great Uncle first mentioned seeing the mysterious light on a previous trip, then it reappeared on a night both he and my brother were fishing the river. My brother described it as a circle of soft light about the size of the bottom of a five-gallon bucket floating slowly over the river. Science suggests these lights are formed by gases released by decaying vegetation in swampy ground. Down at Fort Ancient, the steep hillsides would shelter a gas ball from wind that might otherwise break it apart, allowing it to linger on a muggy summer night. Legend tells a different story, calling them Will o' Wisps or Jack o' Lanterns, claiming they are the ghosts of unbaptized children caught between heaven and hell. Other legends say the lights are the souls of men sold to the devil.

A better place than Fort Ancient, with its ghost town and Indian burial grounds, could not be found for a haunting. There the river travels in long runs and holes suited for catfish, crappies, and sauger fishing, without a lot of the classic smallmouth riffles.

Smallmouth fishing there consists of walking five or ten minutes between riffles and runs, then fishing each one thoroughly. With the exceptional water quality, each spot usually yields some fine fishing, making the effort worthwhile. Also just above the bridge is a large island that provides fine bass fishing as the water pours around it in riffles. Pollution-intolerant caddisfly larvae are common all along this section of river. I've found that in early morning, before the canoe crowd is out in full force, this is a great stretch of river to fish with a fly rod.

The long and smooth heads and tails of each pool are tailor made for a deer hair bug twitched on the surface. This seems to produce some nice-sized fish. I tie a simple deer hair bug as big around as a nickel. I find the best water in the area with a firm bottom of gravel or rock instead of softer muck. For spin fishing, just fish the fastest water you can find that is close to deep water. Fish riffles with a fast moving bait like a spinner or small crankbait early in the day and you will get have success. The fast water provides food and oxygen, the warm temperatures amp up the fish metabolism, and the nearby deep water provides midday sanctuary.

For a few miles on each side of the Fort Ancient Bridge, the hillsides are covered in just about the finest forest remaining in Southwestern Ohio. Early visitors to the Little Miami in the early 1800s described the valley as having the most magnificent forests they had ever encountered. Considering the entire country was cloaked in forest, these woodlands must have been quite majestic to earn such praise.

Along the river just upstream from there, I once found what I'm sure was bobcat scat on the end of a log about chest high off the ground. That was a few years ago. Today, deer are frequently seen crossing the scenic trail in early morning, and the gobbles of wild turkeys ring throughout the woodland. Atop the hillside at the Fort Ancient museum, there are also relics of Paleo-Indians dating back 12,000 years. Large clovis spear points, that would have been used to hunt the mammoths and mastodons that roamed there after the last ice age, can also be seen there. Some mastodon skeletons have been found in Ohio of animals that were eleven feet tall and estimated to have weighed ten thousand pounds. Imagine hunting that with a spear! Other mega-fauna that would have lived in the Little Miami valley in those days would have included the dire wolf, giant beavers, ground sloths, saber toothed cats, and the meanest monster of them all, the short-faced bear. The short-faced bear stood up to twelve feet tall and weighed up to 2500 hundred pounds.

In the earliest years of the 1800s, the woodlands from there upstream to past Waynesville were known for their fine black bear hunting. Although by the end of the 1700s Indians still had villages along the Little Miami, the Hopewell and the Fort Ancient peoples were long gone. The earliest white explorers to Fort Ancient tell of finding mature trees hundreds of years old growing atop the earthworks. One theory holds that the Little Ice Age so devastated Europe from 1300 to the mid-1800s, the Fort Ancient people were influenced to depart from their settled ways into the established woodland culture of the Shawnee. Another theory was that the culture of the Ft. Ancient people was wiped out by disease, introduced by contact with the early Spanish explorers to North America. To me some combination of the two seems logical.

Another great feature of the Ft. Ancient section is easy access from the road, the scenic trail or by boat. There could not be a better location for a first class canoe and kayak livery and public access for launch and takeout for those using their own boats. That, and a long history of family-owned and operated facilities there, explains the successful operation of what is now called Morgan's Outdoor Center. They offer a variety of trips that cover the best of that section of the river, enabling a paddler or fisherman to plan a trip that either begins or ends at their Ft. Ancient facility. Morgan's also operates another location a few miles downstream, called Morgan's Riverside Campground. It has full-service riverside campsites for tent campers, and some small one-room cabins that can turn a day trip into an overnight or weekend.

There is also ample public parking for wade fishermen, with good access to the river walking or on a bike. If you park at the ODNR public parking lot alongside the Rt. 350 bridge, and walk or bike down the scenic trail for a few minutes you will come to a stone bridge over a small creek. The curved arch looks like it should be home to a troll or two.

This small creek has created a nice rock bar out in the river, speeding up the current and providing a

fine area to fish. I usually fish this water fast at first, picking up a fish or two on an inline spinner, then slowing down and going back over the water with a plastic grub or marabou jig or weighted streamer, if fly fishing. Fly fishing using a streamer, or throwing a jig there, has produced white bass, sauger, bass, drum, and at least one decent channel cat.

The Fort Ancient people and the Shawnee, who lived all along the banks of the Little Miami, shared many ways of doing things. Artifacts from both cultures are similar. Many archeologists believe the Shawnee are most likely the true descendants of the Fort Ancient people. Since most of the Scots and Irish settlers of Kentucky and Ohio ended up with traces of Cherokee and Shawnee blood in their genealogy, I like to think so, having the blood of these Scots-Irish hillbillies running in my own veins as well. Maybe some tiny fraction of my own heritage dates back to these people.

Although called Fort Ancient, this place wasn't really a fort at all; the walls are broken by 63 large gateways that would have been impossible to defend. It is thought that instead of a military-type fort, this was the religious center for villages from the surrounding countryside, their Mecca of sorts. I rather like the idea of Fort Ancient as a place of pilgrimage and worship instead of a fort. Any theory that has one of my favorite fishing spots being a holy place makes perfect sense to me.

These ancient peoples would have grown corn and squash there, and gathered wild foods such as ramps or acorns from the surrounding forests. Pearls and shells from the Little Miami were much used in jewelry, and they would have traveled the river in dug-out canoes trapping and catching its plentiful fish. Whether or not their spirits now haunt the river frightening fishermen as glowing balls of light is, of course, another thing entirely.

Downstream of Fort Ancient is Blue Shin. What a great name! I have no evidence of what gives Blue Shin its name but one of the early settlers close to there was a George Shinn, I'm guessing its named after a family member, but if you know better please let me know. Long deep holes and nice riffles dot the river from there, all the way upstream to Ft. Ancient. Morgan's Outdoor Center operates Morgan's Campground there offering great access to some of the river's best fishing. Make no mistake, the outstanding character and quality of the Ft. Ancient section of the river has made it among the most popular for all comers, and it does get crowded on weekends and hot sunny days. However, despite its popularity for family fun and recreation, it remains an excellent stretch for fishing, with a great variety and some big fish. The thing to do is plan your trip to start early, well before the river gets crowded with boats, or late in the day when most are off the river. Also, keep in mind that before Memorial Day and after Labor Day there is usually a lot less boating pressure than during the summer season.

My mother landing a nice fish on the LMR circa 1950s

Morrow and Todd's Fork

"wait without hope, for hope would be hope for the wrong thing"

by T.S.Eliot

Morrow is an excellent place to begin a fishing trip. I've started several trips by enjoying an ice cream cone standing on "the point," downtown at the mouth of Todd's Fork, looking over the Little Miami and the Fork, deciding where to spend the day casting for smallmouth. Unfortunately, as a business and residential community, Morrow seems always to struggle. The ice cream parlor has seemed to be just about the only business not boarded up or run down in downtown Morrow.

The wide street that passes along the beautiful old train depot is often empty, except for a few moms pushing strollers, or maybe an old man sitting on a bucket out on the point, fishing. Other river towns such as South Lebanon and Waynesville are also suffering the effects of economic stress, struggling to hold their own as residential and business communities. That said, it is a good place to plan a paddle trip or fishing trip on some of the best water on the river.

Although I've never witnessed it, local fishing lore has a nice musky caught right there at the mouth of Todd's Fork about every few years. I do know that in winter on a warm day you have a chance to catch some nice sauger there. Some of the biggest sauger I've taken in the river have been caught there.

A plastic grub on a jighead or a minnow are good choices for sauger in the river. They have the odd habit of actually liking some resistance when biting, so using a much heavier jighead than you would use for any other fish can sometimes increase your success rate.

Right on the point, at the confluence of Todd's Fork and the Little Miami River, is the Little Miami Canoe Livery, an establishment that has provided canoe and kayak livery service and rentals for many years. They a also have a livery upstream at Oregonia that makes for a nice paddle, float or fishing day-trip starting at Oregonia and ending at Morrow.

If you ever find yourself out on the point looking out on the river, turn and look up Todd's Fork at the old railroad bridge. Twice I've seen the river pouring over that bridge in floods. Now turn and look directly across the Little Miami at the river bottoms on the far bank. If you follow a line in your mind level with the old railroad bridge you can see why the town of Fredericksburg is no longer there. Just a few old houses remain, including the one that held Cook's bait shop when I was a kid. Before there was even a town of Morrow, Fredericksburg was founded on the far bank just after 1800. Giant floods such as the 1913 flood would cover everything there to the rooftops. Just upstream, before you get to the SR 123 bridge across the river, the first bridge across the Little Miami was built there in 1818. Morrow itself didn't really come into existence as a town until the tracks of the Little Miami River Railroad Company reached there in 1844. For awhile after that, Morrow boomed along with the railroad, then declined with the railroad.

The town of Morrow was named after railroad president Jeremiah Morrow, a two-time Governor of Ohio who was one of Warren County's most famous citizens. Jeremiah Morrow was friends with Thomas Jefferson, James Monroe, and John Quincy Adams. The town of Morrow was a jumping off point for sportsmen riding the train out of Cincinnati, to fish the Little Miami River. My dad worked for the railroad on a section gang out of the Morrow Depot, responsible for the track from the Village of Morrow downstream to Foster.

Just upstream of the SR 123 bridge is the ruins of an old dam and millrace. The first operating mill around there was built on the banks of Todd's Fork by William Smalley. Smalley was captured by Indians twice as a young man; once he was held and lived with them for five years. Later he served as a guide and translator for almost every Army Indian campaign of the period. Records of General St. Clair's campaign along the Little Miami report Smalley shooting 21 Indians in battle. He also served General Mad Anthony Wayne as a translator at the signing of the Treaty of Greenville. William Smalley also guided and hunted for the surveying

party of Col. William Lytle and was paid seventy-five cents a day. Lytle later sold Smalley 600 acres, nine miles up Todd's Fork, for $200, where Smalley built a house and a gristmill and sawmill for $5,265 in 1833. Smalley was infamous for his odd appearance, owing to his Indian captors slicing the rims of his ears away from the rest. These rims hung down off his ears askew for the rest of his life.

A small island splits the river just upstream of downtown Morrow at the ruins of the old mill, creating riffles. Red worms fished on tiny hooks produce big catches of suckers as they move up on the riffles in early spring. Snaring suckers off the riffle was done a lot there in the past also.

I've caught several nice smallmouth there, fishing a rooster tail in the smooth fast water, where the river gathers itself in the tail of the big pool above, before pouring over these riffles. Some years, depending upon how the river has dug out or filled in the hole over the winter, the eddy below the island can produce catfish on chicken livers pitched in and allowed to drift around the eddy on un-weighted hooks.

Right above the riffles and ball fields, on the edge of town stands a mighty sycamore tree. But if you walk a few hundred feet further upstream there is a true giant, a behemoth that must have been growing there long before the town, at a time when mountain lions (called "painters" by early pioneers) and wolves roamed the riverbank. Old records show there was a bounty paid for both in early Warren County history. In William Smalley's time there was also a bounty paid for Indian scalps for a few years during the Indian wars. These bounties varied from $96 to $135 dollars, enough money to buy land for a small farm. Around this giant tree is an ideal spot to catch a big carp on a dough ball or crappies in any brush you can find in this big pool.

The woods along the river there also have a few albino squirrels that I've seen while walking the bike path that follows the old rail bed along the river. The hills rise sharply, and a few small trickles form tiny waterfalls that fall off the steep bank into the river. If you can pick your way down the steep bank without breaking your neck, the mouths of these mini streams form tiny rock bars just big enough for an angler to rest while catching some channel cats. The woods there are especially lovely in spring, as they are covered in wildflowers with dutchmen's breeches and trilliums putting on quite a show. This same time of year the gobbles of wild turkeys also often fill these woods.

Going back to Morrow and heading up Todd's Fork opens up miles of some of the best smallmouth fishing in the state for a wading angler. During summer weekends when canoes fill the river, the relative quiet of Todd's Fork can be a welcome escape. A book could be written on fishing this wonderful stream alone. Just out of Morrow, First Creek joins Todd's Fork almost within sight of town. This delightful little stream has several lovely waterfalls, and was followed by the Shawnee who captured Daniel Boone as they took him to villages in Ohio from Kentucky. Around any wood in this pool is a good place to try for crappies and sunfish.

I have encountered a few Kentucky spotted bass there but not enough to come up with any sort of pattern.

At the head of this big pool begin the riffles of Hall's Creek. Hall's Creek enters the river from the left as you wade upstream amidst an outstanding series of riffles and runs in the river. This is one of those sections of river where you might expect to catch four or five species of fish in a morning using something like a small hair jig or plastic grub. Right at the mouth of Hall's Creek, the river makes a sharp turn and has dug a deep hole known locally as the whirlhole. Along the outside bend the current has

eaten away at the bank forming a large cliff that swallows nest in. Opposite the cliff in early spring, marsh marigolds carpet the river bottom completely in yellow. One morning while walking down to the river I walked up on a young doe standing among the flowers, beams of sunlight streaming the sycamores. It was one of those perfect small moments you never forget.

The whirlhole often yields nice catfish. I'll never forget the big channel cat I caught there on a grub that had me thinking for a minute I'd hooked a record smallmouth. Softcraws or nightcrawlers can be very productive fished there and the run leading down to the whirlhole often yields a nice bass or two to a jig sweeping down with the current. Often while fishing there, I'll search the rock bars thrown up by the river and up Hall's Creek itself for fossils. The whole of the Little Miami watershed is rich in fossils, but a few years ago a cloudburst was centered there that dropped eight inches of rain in a few hours. This caused Hall's Creek and the other nearby creeks to blow out and exposed tons and tons of rock rich in fossils.

The entire Little Miami watershed including tributaries like Todd's Fork and Caesar Creek and Hall's Creek were cut by an even greater flood, the melting of the great glaciers at the end of the last ice age. The torrents of meltwater cut the steep valleys and laid down the gravel beds mined all along the river. As the water cut the valleys of the Little Miami drainage it exposed the layers of rock formed in the Ordovician Age, about 500 million years ago. Then a great shallow sea covered this area and now I often find the fossils of cephalopods there at Hall's Creek. Cephalopods were squid-like creatures that thrived in the ancient sea. Some types of cephalopods were the largest animals of the Ordovician world. Fossils have been found measuring over thirty feet in length. Some that are seven feet long have been found close to there.

Most fossils of cephalopods I find along the river are one-to-three-inch sections of their segmented shells. Once my wife remarked that while doing laundry she never had to look for other women's phone numbers and the like in my pockets, but instead had to watch out for weird things like rocks or pieces of bone. It seems I'm constantly picking up something while bumming around the river.

There at Hall's Creek I've come a mile upstream from Stubb's Mill and usually get out of the river there and hike back down the road to my truck at the old bridge. After all, encountering heron rookeries, Indian mounds, old pioneers, great floods, and fossilized sea monsters, along with the occasional smallmouth bass, makes for a pretty full morning.

Blown to Atoms!
Junction Bridge to Kings Mills

I remember as a youngster walking across the railroad bridge at Middletown Junction.

My father, brother, and I walked down the old tracks of the Middletown and Cincinnati railroad from the direction of Hagerman's crossing, and crossed the bridge here to mushroom hunt in the old abandoned fields at the junction. I say the Middletown and Cincinnati Railroad just because they were the first owner of the line. It was also owned at one time or another by the Cincinnati, Lebanon and Northern railway, the Pennsylvania Railroad, Pennsy's successor the Penn Central, Conrail, and the Indiana and Ohio. The exact dates and order of all that is not clear enough to me to sort out here. All I remember is being a young boy and being afraid to look down between the ties as I walked the bridge. It's now owned by the City of Lebanon and part of the rails to trails program. It's funny but the old bridge still stands and doesn't seem so high now. When the Lebanon Scenic Trail was connected to the Little Miami Scenic Trail, they used the framework of the old bridge to cross the river. But now instead of open ties there is solid blacktop and is much less scary crossing.

The original railroad junction had a triangular shape, to allow trains to travel either direction on the Little Miami Railroad. Now only the leg closest to South Lebanon is paved as bikeway. The other leg is rapidly being retaken by forest, as is the old river bottom we mushroom hunted in. Long before my time, my grandfather farmed corn in this bottom, hauling it in a wagon back up to his house atop Punkin Brown Hill, in South Lebanon. Inside the "Y" is a tangled jungle full of old pieces of rail and iron and stone relics of the railroad. Getting around in here is close to impossible; and I've often said this will be my hideout when I've had enough and become an outlaw.

Below the bridge the river twists and turns in the sharpest series of curves on the river downstream of Fishpot Ford, creating a series of pools and riffles and runs, packed one after the other. This is also the site of the old dam.

I stopped in the wonderful Warren County Historical Society Museum to check some of my facts and the lady that helped me reminisced about swimming at the dam with her husband. It seems everyone of a certain age that grew up in South Lebanon or Kings Mills has a story about the King's dam. I know it was my father's and his brother's favorite place to fish in their youth. My father also said, most times when they got there his grandfather and several other older men were out on the dam fishing for suckers, or rather snaring suckers. The technique was to use a bit of red worm on a tiny hook with one big treble tied right below that. This rig was fished with a big cane pole so that when the sucker nibbled on the worms you could lift straight up with the long pole and hook him.

Mom with a nice sucker caught below the old dam sometime in the 1950s.

Nowadays right above the ruins of the dam is still one of the deepest spots on the river with a fish-holding eddy on each side. Several times I've slipped a dozen night crawlers in my pack with a rest stop here for lunch in mind. While taking a break from wading and casting I'll usually catch a couple drum and maybe a channel cat here. One of those drum is quite likely to be the best fish of the day.

One of the nice things about the fishing here is the fact you might catch four or five species of fish in a morning. This big hole would still be a great place to catch a big flathead if you spent the night here. Nowadays you would have to make the commitment to spend the whole night as the path down from the scenic trail would be awful in the dark. The old fields have grown up in an impenetrable thicket. I've been unable to find out when the dam was built. In 1878 Joseph Warren King and his nephew Ahimaaz King bought the property of a gristmill located there, all ready to construct powder mills along the millrace running through their new purchase. The water in the race was used both to power the mills and to fight the fires from the inevitable explosions.

If you look at the photo above, it shows a closeup of a piece of the old dam. You can see that under the concrete is an older layer made up of stones laid side by side on edge. I wonder if this was the old milldam and was covered in concrete by the powder mills. Up by the scenic trail, the foundation of the old keg shop where powder kegs were built is slowly disappearing in the undergrowth.

My father says in the old days this was a place to bring home a mess of channel cats by fishing chicken liver under a float through the twists and turns. Though I haven't yet tried it, I imagine it still is. I don't know if this is an exceptional place for wildlife, or if I've just been lucky, but it seems like I see a fox or a muskrat or a mink every time I fish here. I know this was one of my father's favorite places to trap for mink back in the day. Last week I rounded a rock bar there, and a big softshell turtle came hurtling down the bank and across the sand, splashing into the river. When I walked up to where she spooked I could see her tracks leading back to where she had dug a hole into the sand and laid a clutch of eggs. Downstream the river straightens again and you can see the bridge abutments of the powder line bridge used by the Peters Cartridge Company. Here and below in the "Dry House Hole" there is deep water made for catfishing.

The original Kings factory, built in the 1860s, made bullets for the Union Army during the Civil War, and was a target for Morgan's Raiders during their 1863 trip through Ohio, though the Raiders never made it to the factory.

The company sequestered much of the more dangerous parts of its gunpowder manufacturing operation into smaller buildings up and down the river, after the explosion on July 15, 1890. At 3:50p.m., a train car collided with two cars loaded with 800 kegs of black powder. This set off a chain reaction that exploded another 800 plus kegs of powder and thousands of shells leveling the main factory in a blast heard all over the countryside. Papers all over the country carried news of what must have then been one of the world's biggest explosions. One paper's headline read "BLOWN TO ATOMS!" as no traces of several workers were ever found.

On a rock bar there remains a set of train wheels from this or one of the other explosions that happened over the years. The riffle with the train wheels I called "the Drowning Run," as I was swept off my feet here wading one fishing trip, and was pretty bruised, beat up and half-drowned before I made it out.

The factory was rebuilt after the company sued and won a lawsuit for damages against the Little Miami Railroad. The shot tower, where the tiny molten lead shotgun pellets were dropped to form round pellets, was for decades the tallest structure in Warren County, until the replica Eiffel Tower was built at Kings Island Amusement Park. Most of the smaller buildings are fading back into the woods now, and even the large factory is mostly a giant ruin, even though it is listed in the National Register of Historic Places.

Among the graffiti painted on ruins are several pentagrams or five-sided stars. While most of these were painted by kids, local legend has several satanic rituals taking place in the ruins of the old factory. These stories, along with the deaths of workers, have the old powder plant being listed high on any list of Ohio's haunted places. Add the Native American burial mounds all up and down the river, the tragedy at Mather's Mill, and the strange lights at Ft. Ancient, and the Little Miami might be the most haunted river on earth. During the great depression in the 1930s, Peters sold out to Remington, its competitor. Among my most treasured possessions is my grandfather's ring presented to him for twenty-five years of service to the company.

In recent years attempts have been made to restore the historic building of Peters Cartridge by a number of developers. Today the complex is owned by Dupont. In 2014, as a Superfund site, the company is working with U.S. EPA to clean up lead-contaminated soils. The riverfront forest between the river and trail are owned by the Little Miami Conservancy as a permanent nature preserve.

South Lebanon

"At a certain season of our life,
we are accustomed to consider
every spot as the possible site
of a house."

by Henry David Thoreau

The miles between the campground riffle at Morrow and the Junction bridge below South Lebanon are as close to home water as it comes for me.

Every grown male in four generations of our family has fished there. Most are buried somewhere in this watershed. And the heart of this home stretch is South Lebanon. South Lebanon is ideally suited as a base for fishing the river. Good access, good water, and the comfort that comes with the familiar. The new Oeder Park and the rebirth of Turtle Creek's water quality have combined to make these the "good old days" for fishing in South Lebanon.

South Lebanon started out as Deerfield, and is actually the oldest town in Warren County. The town was laid out in 1795, and lots were given away to entice people to settle and clear land. After 29 lots were given away, the rest of the lots were sold for two dollars each on average, though records show a James Cory bought three lots for a grand total of five dollars. Around 1800, Deerfield was the most im-

portant place north of Cincinnati, as early pioneers often left their families there as they cleared farms in wilder places up and down the river.

Deerfield/South Lebanon has been home to some extraordinary business ventures, such as one of the first canning operations in the country. In my youth, I can also remember the buildings of the old "mushroom factory," that raised mushrooms there until mushroom farming in old mines became popular. My own family ran a large fur operation and bought fur from hunters and trappers for miles around. South Lebanon also was famous as the home of Cash's Big Bargain Barn, a furniture store run by the fundamentalist preacher Cash D. Amburgy. Family legend has it that my great grandfather threatened to kill Cash, because my grandmother was a member of an early church that practiced snake handling and Grandfather was afraid for her safety.

Probably South Lebanon's most famous resident was one of its first. David Sutton was one of Deerfield's earliest settlers and became Warren County's first clerk of courts. During the War of 1812 he raised a company of soldiers and rose through the ranks, becoming a general in the militia. He also served in the legislature in 1816, 1818, and 1823. He died in 1834 and was buried in Deerfield. He also ran a tavern on one of those two-dollar lots. I sometimes wonder what he would think of people wading the same river he knew, with hundred-dollar fishing poles throwing five-dollar lures.

A semi-conductor manufacturing plant, high on the hill overlooking the Little Miami River used to legally discharge waste water that contained copper and ammonia into Turtle Creek, which in turn flows into the Little Miami River there at South Lebanon. Back in those days the government would study the operation of a manufacturing or processing facility, and issue an NPDES permit (stands for National Pollutant Discharge Elimination System), legalizing a certain level of discharge of chemicals from its operation, even though it would end up in the Little Miami River, or the Ohio River, or some other river. Finally in 1998, the semi-conductor plant in South Lebanon ceased operating, and quit discharging into Turtle Creek. A 2007 study of the river by the EPA, using their scale which measures the ability of the physical habitat to support a biotic community, now rates the Little Miami through my home waters as anywhere from excellent to exceptional. Less than a decade ago these waters would have rated half as well.

A two-minute walk from the park, and you can cross Turtle Creek watching minnows skip wildly as smallmouth chase them up on the rock bar. A white or silver rooster tail fished straight out from the mouth of Turtle Creek is on the money.

Turtle Creek was named not for plentiful turtles, but named after the war Chief Little Turtle of the Miami Indians. General Josiah Harmar, leading an army of mostly malacia, marched up the Little Miami River in a mostly unsuccessful bid to quell the Indians in 1790. He tried, but could not defeat Little Turtle. The following year, Little Turtle defeated a much better armed and organized army led by General Arthur St. Clair. General Mad Anthony Wayne marched a third army up the Little Miami, and finally fared much better, defeating the Indians at the Battle of Fallen Timbers. Later in life, Little Turtle preached peace with the U.S. and even met George Washington in 1797.

From the mouth of Turtle Creek looking downriver you can see just ahead the big bridge where State Route 48 crosses the river. The water between Turtle Creek and the bridge is way too shallow for quality fishing when the river is in its best shape, but is a great place to cross. I usually head across and down to the bridge, for right below the bridge starts a fine run. River right looking downstream has a broken rocky bottom and in July and August gets a lot of shade early in the afternoon. A little too deep for a spinner or Rapala there, so I mostly fish an 1/8 ounce jighead and plastic grub. The first hundred

yards below the bridge has consistently produced some of my best river smallmouth. My dad says this stretch of river was called the "stoneygrounds" and was a popular fishing and camping spot. Nowadays I pretty much have it to myself.

River left there is a broad long shallow rock bar that I wade while casting across river to the far bank. I continually find myself poking around on this shallow bar trying to wade as softly as I can to watch the multitude of minnows streaming by underfoot. My father also says in the old days you could seine dozens of crayfish from a shallow river bar like this. For many years this was no longer the case but now this rock bar is simply covered in crayfish. Turn over two or three rocks, and one or two inch long crayfish will shoot away backwards to hide again a few feet further on. The explosion of life in the river there has mostly taken place in just the last few years, as the improving water quality has jumped off the charts.

Oeder Park isn't the only easy access to the river in South Lebanon by a long shot. Upstream at Rogers Park there is a canoe access with ample parking to fish the riffles around the big island in the river.

Looking back across Rogers Park towards town in summer, with the river knee deep, it's hard to imagine the big floods that covered the hundreds of yards across the ball fields and up into South Lebanon along there. Growing up along the river, I have seen water up across the ball fields and into town, but nothing like the big flood where my father rode all through town in a canoe. The really huge flood of 1913 that took out bridges and destroyed homes and lives there has kept the riverbank mostly ball fields and park, and has, in a way, protected the river from the town.

Across the river where the old train depot once stood, there is more parking for the scenic trail that follows that side of the river. The old railroad dumped literally hundreds of tons of concrete and rock rubble into the river there to protect the rail line from erosion. These stones and slabs range from basketball to car-size and give this section of river its name "the big rocks". The extreme downstream end of the big rocks has several rock bars that jut straight out into the river, and each has a strong eddy behind that's home to some pumpkin seeds and channel cats. The seam where this eddy hits current holds a few smallmouth and sauger when

Dad with a large catfish sometime in the 1950s.

the river is in good shape, and once provided me a three pound smallie on an inline spinner. Upstream, the river deepens in front of the big rocks and the current, depth and cover are home to smallmouth and rock bass. There I throw a small crankbait or spinner with small trebles instead of single hooked lures like jigs or grubs, because panfish and rock bass are as common a catch as bass. I've heard old timers used to fish there free-lining a minnow with a long cane pole, catching bass and catfish.

Foster

Foster (sometimes given as Fosters) is an unincorporated community in Southern Warren County, Ohio, United States. It straddles the Little Miami River in Deerfield and Hamilton Townships. It is located about two miles southwest of Hopkinsville, two miles west of Maineville, and two miles northeast of Twenty Mile Stand, just off State Routes 22/3, the 3C Highway. In the 1930s, the State of Ohio erected a new high bridge over the river that bypassed the community.

The once booming town of Foster was named after the Foster family. It was a quaint little town right on the river where the recently renamed "George Terwilliger Bridge" now spans the Little Miami River. James H. Foster came to the area in 1841 or 1842 and built a mill and hotel on the east side of the river. Soon there were 48 businesses and houses crammed in between the steep hillsides that flank the Little Miami there. These included a sawmill, cobblers, hotel, blacksmith shop, and five bars. Forty seven buildings and five bars! Now that's what I call a wild river town.

In the late 1800's, Foster was a popular destination for picnics, fishing and relaxing. Around 1886 Augustine Hoppe bought the mill and the land enclosed by the millrace was called Hoppe's Island. There were picnic tables and a park-like atmosphere.

According to old reports you had to show up at daylight to get a picnic table on a weekend. This is likely true, because in the late 1940s Hoppe's Island had been renamed Glenn Island, and turned into an amusement park of sorts with a swimming pool and a beach that allowed patrons to swim either in the river, at the beach, or in a bankside swimming pool.

The same parcel of real estate is now owned and operated by the Ohio Department of Natural Resources as a public watercraft access and park. Now named the Carl A. Rahe Public Access, (formerly Glenn Island Public Access), it is located about 0.2 mile downstream of the Terwilliger Bridge, on the right descending bank. This public access is a perfect launch point for a fishing trip from Foster to Loveland.

Today, the riffle and runs that are split by the island offer a place to wade fish right there, or launch a kayak or canoe to begin the 4 ½ mile float to Loveland. If you like to walk in the woods, the wooded part of the Carl Rahe Access property, downstream of the parking lot, still contains recognizable ruins of the old concrete steps, and ruins that are the remains of the old Glenn Island Amusement Park.

The Foster's Viaduct, a tall bridge of historic design, spans the gorge bypassing the tiny town, pret-

tolerant species are found there, including a large number of caddisfly larvae. It is decent fishing for smallmouth bass, sauger, and carp.

Upstream of Foster, the river makes a sharp curve creating a rocky bar and riffle and the fishing is much better. It is about a ten-minute walk, but worth the trouble. This was one of my uncle's favorite spots, and he used to tell me tales of catching lots of channel cats there on chicken liver. Although I haven't

ty much putting Foster out of business as a viable community. Now, only the Train Stop Inn bar and a couple other buildings remain. The riffle right below the viaduct is one of the fishiest looking fishing spots on the river, but is also one of the most fished, and easiest spots to get to, so the fishing is only hit and miss. Large rocks, gravel and boulders make up the river bottom in this big riffle, and the hard bottom continues quite a ways on down the river. There was also once a dam the remains of which were removed some 25 years ago. The nice gravel and rapids means you will find a wide variety of macro invertebrates present. Many pollution-in-

fished there much for smallmouth, I did try it three times last year and did well each time on a 1/8th ounce jighead and plastic grub. For an ambitious paddler, this is another place where an upstream paddle of about one mile, through relatively slack water can get you into some excellent water for fly fishing or spin casting. However, this entire area, between Foster and Kings Mill, has the potential to be some of the best bass fishing on the river, and I plan to spend a lot more time there in the future.

Loveland

To my eyes, Loveland may be the prettiest town on the whole river. It is, at least, the one who's made the biggest attempt to embrace its heritage as a river town. Indeed, even though the bikeway runs the length of the river, I've heard several people refer to it as the Loveland bike path no matter where all along its length they mention. And no wonder, since here, restaurants, ice cream shops, bike shops, coffee and tea shops, and the LMC Scenic River & Trail Center line the trail through town.

Right in town at the mouth of O'Bannon Creek may not be the best place to start your fishing adventures on the Little Miami. Not because it's not fishy looking but because it's crawling with kids wading, dogs fetching, and people just generally enjoying the river. Upstream at the first riffle before the really deep water begins will always be special to me, for here I lost the biggest smallmouth I've ever hooked.

It was late fall when the bass hit a grub and jumped clean out of the water giving me a good look at its size. I had the big bass on long enough to be sure I was going to land it when the line just went slack. No theatrics, just a slack line and no fish. A few kids were watching from downstream and it was all I could do not to throw a mini hissyfit in midstream. Not that it would have helped any. I won't say what I thought the bass weighed so I won't be called a liar, let's just call it very large.

Loveland is named after James Loveland, who ran a store and post office near the railroad tracks downtown. The railroad promoted Loveland as a resort town and gave it the nickname "Little Switzerland

of the Miami Valley." In the 1920s, the *Cincinnati Enquirer* ran a promotion that offered a free plot of land in Loveland, along the Little Miami River, for a one-year subscription to the paper! The *Enquirer* also played a role in the creation of Loveland's most famous attraction, *Château Laroche*, or just simply, The Loveland Castle. The Castle is a huge replica of a medieval castle built on the Little Miami by Harry Andrews starting in 1929. Harry was a Boy Scout leader and spent a lifetime adding to the castle. The Castle is built on two free lots of land that his scouts obtained by selling one-year subscriptions to the *Cincinnati Enquirer*. It's amazing and worth a trip in its own right to see. And like any good castle it is supposedly haunted.

Speaking of hauntings and the paranormal, I almost forgot to mention that mythical monster that haunts the Little Miami along here, the fearsome Loveland Frog or maybe lizard depending on who you talk to, though the most popular version has the monster named the Loveland Frog. A barely humanoid creature with green skin all bumpy and hideous like (you guessed it) a frog! Oh and bulging eyes and a huge frog mouth too.

According to *Wikipedia*: "The first claimed sighting was in May 1955. A businessman is said to have seen three or four 3-foot (0.91 m)-tall frog-faced creatures squatting under a bridge near Loveland. They were described as having wrinkles instead of hair on their heads, lopsided chests, and wide mouths without lips, like frogs. One of them is said to have held up a bar device that shed sparks. A strong odor of alfalfa and almonds was reportedly left behind."

So there you have it, it's on the internet so it has to be true. The fearsome frog has been seen off and on ever since, even to the point of being shot at by the police as it fled back into its home, the Little Miami. And (yes there's more) the frog even has its own page on *Monsterquests*, the TV show's own website, and a Google search turns up around 100,000 results, more "proof positive" that the slimy reptilian haunts the waters of the Little Miami. The Miami Indians and their allies the Shawnee that lived along the Little Miami also had a legend about the Shawnahooc or "River Demon" that lived along the river who just happened to look a lot like a lizard or frog. Coincidence? I think not. And while it may be okay to keep a few crappies or channel cats for dinner, Shawnahooc, I've heard, is fond of the river's smallmouth and you run the risk of invoking his wrath if you keep any smallmouth. I dunno, something about it taking three or four years for a smallmouth to mature and recruitment and conserving the resource. It sounds to me like it's best to release all smallmouth from the river just to be safe.

No description of Loveland would be complete without mention of Loveland Canoe and Kayak, formerly known as the Bruce's Canoe Rental.

A beautiful old house right on the river is home base to a fine, well-run boat livery and shuttle service. They offer a variety of canoes and kayaks, as well as tubes and rafts. Their trips start as far up as Foster and even South Lebanon, most terminating at their Loveland home base. However, they also offer trips that begin at Loveland and end downstream at Branch Hill, or even as far down as Milford. Fishing either upstream or down from Loveland can be quite good

Milford

One of the oldest towns around, Milford was built on a survey belonging to John Nancarrow, a Revolutionary War veteran from Virginia. Nancarrow owned 230 acres but never lived in Milford. In money trouble, he sold his land to Phillip Gatch in 1802 for $920.00. In 1806 Gatch sold 125 acres to Ambrose Ransom, and two days later Ransom sold 64 1/2 acres to John Hageman. John Hageman was the first permanent settler and named this area

Hageman's Mills, after a small mill he set up in 1803. By 1815, Hageman had moved west and the name Milford was in common use. The name says it all. Milford was the first safe ford north of Cincinnati. The water is still shallow there with extensive rock bars all up and down this stretch of river. There is ample parking and river access near the American Legion and at Terrell Park, land purchased by the Little Miami River Conservancy years ago and donated to the City as a river access and nature preserve. LMC and the City have recently established another nature preserve above the bridge at the old Clermont Lumber site.

Here the river, with all its riffles and rock bars, has great smallmouth fishing and is ideal to wade. Downstream, deeper riffles provide excellent habitat for dobsonfly larvae and stonefly nymphs. Below the town of Milford to the river's confluence with the East Fork of the LMR is some of the best big smallmouth water on the River. The East Fork, running from East Fork Lake's dam all the way to Milford, also offers great fishing and you could fill a book on this exceptional stream alone.

Upstream of Milford, at Fletcher Road, the scenic trail crosses the river on a high railroad trestle known as the Hippie Bridge, because of the graffiti and the fact that it has been a party spot for young folks. There is fine fishing there for all the fish in the river, as the river varies widely within a quarter mile up and downstream of Hippie Bridge.

Armleder Park

East of downtown Cincinnati just off State Route 125 on Old Wooster is a jewel in the Hamilton County park system, Otto Armleder Memorial Park. Over three hundred acres of soccer fields, dog parks, and roller-blading trails hide the fact that the whole backside of the park stretches along the Little Miami River. And not just any stretch of river, but a very interesting one containing a number of bends, riffles, and the biggest rock bars on the river. Unfortunately for the fishing, proximity to the dog park means there is often a Labrador retriever splashing up and down the riverbank. Get there early in the morning, before people come pouring into the park, and enjoy some of the best fishing on the whole river, especially for that piscatorial dinosaur, the gar.

Armleder's extensive shallows, with a rock instead of muddy bottom, are prime territory to catch one of these scary monsters. That long bony bill, filled with sharp teeth, makes a gar very hard to hook with conventional techniques. I use medium spinning tackle and cut bait. The trick is to cut the bait into a one-inch squares and use a small hook. Use just enough weight to keep the bait in place, or even none if possible. The bait is cast out and the bail left open and the line secured by a tiny rock so the gar can pick up the bait and run with it. Typically the fish will take off on a lightning-fast run and you need to wait. And wait, and wait, and wait. It's almost impossible to wait too long to strike when gar fishing. You want the fish to swallow the bait, as it's nearly impossible to land one otherwise. They are strong and able fighters and I've had them jump completely out of the water during the battle. By the way, don't use a stainless steel hook as you are just going to cut the line to release the fish. The enzymes inside the gars stomach will dissolve the hook rather quickly. Almost any fish hooked deeply has a much better chance of survival if you cut the line, rather than try to rip the hook out, inevitably causing injury.

Armleder has wide, shallow stretches that are not great fish holding spots, but the bends hold all the major fish species in the river. The shallow riffles and bends fill with white bass during the great spring white bass run, and huge catches of fish are possible. There's also a very nice, little known canoe launch

that will let you explore more of the river too. The huge gravel and rock bars make Armleder a super destination in the spring and late summer, when wading birds are migrating. A nice shaded trail following the riverbank lets you imagine you are in wilder country, offering fine river views to fishermen and birders.

Magrish River Lands Preserve

If you're roaring across the Little Miami on Kellogg Avenue and see the sign for Salem Road, take it. Down around the looping exit ramp you turn left into the Magrish River Lands Preserve, less than a minute away from the hustle and bustle of the big city. Magrish itself is a 45 acre preserve that butts up against California Woods on one side and the opposite river bank belongs, the best I can tell, to Lunken Airport. The river flows beneath the Kellogg Avenue bridge, past a harbor busy with boat traffic from the Ohio River, then out to the main stem of Ohio River. Upstream of that lies Magrish, and quiet, quiet, quiet. Well almost.

Just when you think you are away from the big city, here comes a plane from nearby Lunken Airport, buzzing overhead. The airport makes up for that though (almost) by helping keep Magrish a little bit isolated and off the beaten path. You might share the place with a lone birdwatcher, but you're just as likely to have the place completely to yourself, at least during the week. And even though you're in the city, there's somehow a lot of empty space to have completely to yourself, because for a long ways upstream there is nothing in the floodplain.

Up river toward SR125 I caught the largest fish I've ever caught out of the Little Miami, a huge carp I guesstimated at somewhere between thirty-five and forty pounds.

Folks who live nearby and fish the river daily tell me the fish seem to wander in and out of the Ohio River ranging up the Little Miami quite a ways. This makes for quite a bit of mystery and surprise. One day the river there is full of fish, the next, seemingly empty. But this also makes for diversity, with white bass schooling one day and something different like hybrid stripers the next.

The history of this place is really the history of Cincinnati itself, for one of the city's original settlers, Benjamin Stites, settled there on 20,000 acres. Stites owned the riverbank from the mouth to upstream of present day Lunken Airport. He was a trader who seemed to buy and sell a bit of everything. When a band of Shawnee stole his horses and some goods near Washington, Kentucky, a party set off to try and recover them, following the Shawnee across the Ohio and up the Little Miami. Supposedly, Stites was so taken by the beauty of the Little Miami River valley that he decided then and there that he would-someday settle there.

Sites helped persuade John Cleves Symmes, a New Jersey Congressman, to purchase territory between the Miamis from the federal government, divide it into parcels, and sell the land to settlers such as himself. In 1787, Symmes contracted with the United States Treasury Board to buy one million acres of the region. Symmes' first buyer was, of course, Stites. And the rest, as they say, is history. Being subject to floods of both the Ohio and Little Miami rivers has kept this location as peaceful as possible while the great city of Cincinnati has grown all around it.

The Little Miami Railroad

Possibly the one thing man has done to most affect the river has been to build the railroad. Indeed, several of the small towns up and down the river owe their very existence to the railroad. And with the railroad's decline and eventual closing, so have the fortunes of these small towns declined.

Incorporated in 1836, the railroad was conceived as the best way to get goods from the capital and central Ohio to Cincinnati and the Ohio River. This was considered so important to the state's future that the railroad's first president was Governor Jeremiah Morrow, who served without pay. In 1837 there was a great economic crisis, and the fledgling railroad was unable to buy steel rails, so the first bit of track laid actually used wooden rails for a year.

The track reached Milford in 1841 and Loveland a year later. Tracks were laid to Xenia in 1845 and Springfield in 1846, a full decade after the company was formed. There the railroad met the track of the Columbus & Xenia railroad, and central and northern Ohio were finally linked to the Ohio River. For decades, the Little Miami River Railroad was said to be one of the most profitable railroads in the world. Over time, though, as the country spread westward, north/south rail lines began to lose their importance to east/west lines, and the Little Miami Railroad (LMRR) declined in importance.

In 1870 the LMRR was merged into the Pennsylvania Railroad. The LMRR was operated by the Pennsy until that railroad too eventually declined, went bankrupt, and merged into Conrail. With the merger, the line was idled except for a few miles closest to Cincinnati which are still in use today. For years the track was unused, until it was ultimately converted to recreational use as the wonderful Little Miami Scenic Trail (actually now an Ohio State Park), that follows the rail bed the length of the main stem of the Little Miami River.

My great grandfather, several uncles, my great uncle, and my father all worked for the railroad one time or another. Even in their day, though, the railroad had already passed its glory days, and stations at South Lebanon and Kings Mills had already been closed. My father said he remembers the mail sack hung on a pole in South Lebanon to be snagged by the trains as they passed without stopping.

Miles and miles of riverbank have been profoundly affected by the railroad as thousands of tons of rock and rubble were dumped along the riverbank by the railroad to control erosion. Probably the best places to see this are just north of South Lebanon at the "Big Rocks" and at Foster. My grandfather had an extensive collection of old glass and ceramic insulators that had been left on telegraph poles alongside the abandoned track. Several of these old poles can still be seen poking out of the bushes all along the scenic trail. Other neat old reminders of the railroad's glory days are the wonderful old stations kept up by towns like Yellow Springs or Loveland as well as old markers or signal and water towers at such places as Fort Ancient and Roxanna. The Little Miami River was marketed by the railroad as a

sportsman's paradise, and excursions were offered to fishermen from Cincinnati to towns like Loveland and South Lebanon. Even now the old rail bed offers access to many thousands of fishermen, hikers, bikers, and birdwatchers every year who use the scenic trail to see the wonders of the river. In 1980 the Little Miami Conservancy successfully pushed for federal and state funding from the newly created Rails to Trails program to allow the Ohio DNR to purchase 45 miles of the rail line and begin its conversion to the present multi-use recreational trail. Today, the trail is mostly an Ohio State Park, substantially maintained by volunteers, and enjoyed by an estimated 350,000 visitors every year.

The Little Miami Scenic Trail

The beautiful Little Miami Scenic Trail is known to many as one of the most pleasant places to spend a day anywhere, and draws bikers, walkers, fisherman, birdwatchers and more by the thousands every year. That is why, to be both technically and politically correct, you should always refer to it as the Little Miami State Park Multi-Purpose Trail. Following close alongside the beautiful Little Miami River, it offers a chance to see nature at its finest. Stretching 78 miles from Springfield to Newtown, there are countless places to get away from it all while still being in reach of the charming ice cream shops and restaurants that grace the many small towns the trail passes through. The section of the Little Miami Scenic Trail in Clark County is operated by the Clark County Park District, and the National Trail Parks and Recreation District. Due to budget concerns parts of this northernmost section have sometimes been closed.

From the trailhead in Springfield, Ohio, the Little Miami Trail runs south to Yellow Springs, home to Antioch College and the must-see Glen Helen Nature Preserve. "The Glen" is home to the large yellow-colored spring that gives the town its name and visitors can view lovely wildflowers, huge old trees, cliffs with waterfalls, rock overhangs and an historic covered bridge. Nearby are Clifton Gorge State Nature Preserve and John Bryan State Park, two of the most scenic areas in the United States. Located along the Little Miami National Wild & Scenic River, Clifton Gorge is famous for its waterfalls and rapids that flow through a narrow gorge. Close to John Bryan State Park, the North Country Trail and Buckeye Trail enter from the west and Dayton. For the next 15 miles South to Spring Valley, the Little Miami trail is managed by Greene County. At Xenia Station, it meets the Creekside Trail, and the Prairie Grass Trail, on which the Ohio to Erie Trail continues north toward Columbus, Ohio. Little Miami State Park (nothing changes but the name) begins at Hedges Road in Spring Valley and follows U.S. 42 south into Warren County. It passes through Corwin (near Waynesville, Caesar Creek State Park, and Oregonia), where the Buckeye Trail rejoins. Corwin and Waynesville are home to several nice places to take a break from the trail. There, you can enjoy antique and specialty shops that dot the towns, or have a good meal in one of the restaurants.

South of Waynesville the trail enters another wooded gorge and passes close by the lovely Corwin M. Nixon covered bridge, possibly the prettiest covered bridge you will ever see. At Fort Ancient, the trail runs under the awesome twin Jeremiah Morrow Bridges and Interstate 71. These bridges are 239 feet above the river, and are the tallest bridges in Ohio. They are 2300 feet long, spanning the Little Miami's huge wooded gorge containing some of the nicest forests along the river's length. The trail then passes through the towns of Morrow and South Lebanon to the Middletown Junction, where the Lebanon Countryside Trail splits off the main trail and runs 7 miles all the way to downtown Lebanon.

Continuing downstream past the Lebanon junction, the river remains on your right as the Little Miami trail continues south, past Kings Mills. At this location the historic Peters Cartridge Company factory overlooks the scenic trail. The huge tower of the Peters factory is unmistakable and can be seen for miles, except in the rich foliage of summer. The site of several tragic accidents over its many years of operation, the Peters facility is reputed to be among Ohio's most haunted places! From there, continuing downstream with the river on your right, the trail passes under U.S. 22/State Route 3 at Foster, traveling beneath one of the prettiest bridges in the country, the Foster's Viaduct. Beyond that it continues downstream, entering Clermont County and beautiful Loveland, Ohio, where for many years it has been known locally as The Loveland Bike Trail.

From Loveland downstream along the Little Miami River, the trail proceeds into the Hamilton County section of the river as it meets State Route 126 (Glendale–Milford Road). The trail passes by Camp Dennison, and its former southern terminus in Milford. A 2006 expansion now continues the trail downstream along Wooster Pike to Terrace Park. From there, the Loveland section of the Buckeye Trail splits off, going to Eden Park in Cincinnati. A short Hamilton County Park District extension brings the Little Miami trail back across the river to the Bass Island river access at Newtown.

The Hamilton County Park District intends to extend the Little Miami Scenic Trail to Clear Creek. From there, it will follow the Little Miami River to a crossing at the Beechmont Avenue bridge and connect to the Lunken Airport and Armleder Park Bike Trails. The Little Miami Scenic Trail follows the right-of-way of the old Little Miami Railroad, maintained by the Ohio Department of Natural Resources as Little Miami State Park. The long, narrow park passes though four counties, with a right-of-way about 50 miles long and roughly 65 feet wide for a total of about 700 plus acres.

The Scenic Trail is another instance in which early efforts of the Little Miami Conservancy (LMC) deserve credit for beginning what we have today. In 1980 LMC successfully pushed for Federal and State funding from the newly created Rails to Trails program to allow Ohio DNR to purchase 45 miles of the rail line that began its conversion to today's multi-use trail.

The LMC actually had to raise the private funds to purchase the southern two miles of the railroad property that ran between Terrace Park downstrem to Plainville when local officials pressed to stop that purchase with public funds. The LMC defended its title to the land in court in the early 1980s before the property was eventually sold by the LMC to the Hamilton County Park District.

Along that stretch of the river corridor the LMC also purchased the Avoca Park and Bass Island properties over a fifteen year period, cleaning up the trashed properties and selling them to the Hamilton County Park District. At the 2006 dedication ceremony of this portion of the trail then-Governor Robert Taft praised LMC for it hard work and vision. ***Today, an estimated 350,000 visitors enjoy the trail every year.***

Mileage Chart Little Miami Bike Trail

Select a starting point on one column and an ending point in another for example it is seven miles from Xenia to Spring Valley. ————————➤

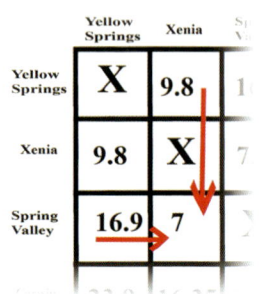

	Yellow Springs	Xenia	Spring Valley	Corwin	Morrow	Loveland	Milford	Springfield
Yellow Springs	X	9.8	16.9	23.9	38.6	52.1	61.6	10
Xenia	9.8	X	7.0	16.25	28.9	43.0	52.0	19
Spring Valley	16.9	7	X	7.1	21.7	35.2	44.7	26.9
Corwin	23.9	16.25	7.1	X	14.7	28.2	37.7	33.9
Morrow	38.6	28.9	21.7	14.7	X	13.5	23	48.6
Loveland	52.1	43	35.2	28.2	13.5	X	9.5	62.9
Milford	61.6	52	44.7	37.7	23	9.5	X	72
Springfield	10	19	26.9	33.9	48.6	62.1	72	X

Fishing With Edgar

I walked up to the desk at the retirement center and mumbled incoherently, the way I often do around strangers in such instances. I'd certainly starve if I had to make a living as a salesman. I muttered something about writing a book on fishing the river, and wanting to talk to someone about how it used to be. The lady just stared at me for a long time. I couldn't tell if she hadn't heard me, or was thinking of calling the cops. Then suddenly she was in motion; "Yeah, come on," she said over her shoulder, and led me down a hallway to a room.

She introduced me to Edgar, and left. I just kind of stood there for a second or two, and then took a few moments to explain to Edgar I just wanted to talk fishing, and wasn't trying to sell him something. After feeling each other out, and trying to find a connection in the way country people do when they first meet, we established that Edgar's father had certainly worked with my grandfather at the Peters Cartridge Company in Kings Mills. Then Edgar relaxed and began to talk fishing.

Edgar grew up on Shawhan Road above South Lebanon, and had fished the river off and on for three quarters of a century. He said his earliest memories of fishing the river were tagging along with his older brother Earl and his cousin Bob catfishing at night. Edgar had a small radio by his bed, and must listen to country music because he said, "You know that song where that fella's wife leaves him for fishing? Well, Bob sounded just like that fella in the song-- "aawwww lookie, there I got a bite."

According to Edgar, they fished with large stout poles made of cane they bought at Browning's Hardware in South Lebanon. The reel and the guides were then taped to the cane with old-fashioned electrical cloth "friction" tape. He said he didn't fish on those trips, and he thought looking back they let him tag along so he could gather firewood. He still remembers the excitement of being on the river around the fire at night back then. Edgar said they went to a nearby field and picked field corn and boiled it in the minnow bucket over the fire. I asked him if they caught any big fish and he said, "God almighty they caught some whoppers!" Some of it may have been his youth, but the "yellowcats" looked as long as him; they used chub minnows for bait, and also set jingle lines up and down the river from sycamore branches.

I asked him if they baited the jingle lines with chubs, and he said mostly, but they also used nightcrawlers and crawdads on the jingle lines, but you had to bait with nightcrawlers right at dark to keep the little fish from pecking them off. He said they caught chubs with a cane pole from the creek up from Stubbs Mills (Bigfoot Run), and from Hall's Creek; that just up from the river was a big pothole in Hall's Creek they could always catch bait in.

Edgar said they would go down the hill on a wagon path and cut across the river bottom to just below Stubbs Mills. There they often kept a skiff and would gig fish by lantern light. Edgar said a man he called Mr. Brent would come up from Cincinnati to Morrow on the train, and would buy bait from Edgar and borrow the skiff. Just below the Stubbs Mills bridge was a small hole in that shallow section, and Mr. Brent would anchor the skiff and fish minnows for bass and channel cat in that hole. Mr. Brent also sometimes would drive up from Cincinnati and would arrive in a coat, hat, and a tie. He would never take off the tie till he had bought bait. Never, he said, you could bank on it. He would buy his bait, take off that tie, and open one of the beers he had in a bucket with ice in his trunk, and go fishing.

The nurse stuck her head in to check on Edgar and said something about not staying too long, but Edgar cut her off. "Dammit woman, can't you see I've got company? Get the hell out!" I promised her I would leave soon. When she left, Edgar's expression softened, and he said she never would let him cuss, till he was dying. I was at a loss for words at that, but it didn't matter, as Edgar jumped right back into his story.

He said they had a big homemade wire trap that they caught crawdads in using rotten fish for bait. That people always loved eating the craws, but he always smelled the rotten fish in his head and couldn't eat them. I asked him about spinning tackle and he said he remembers that DuPont was the only company that made monofilament, and he owned a Mitchell 300, and a grey cardinal with a drag on the top of the reel housing in the back. That he still has the 300 in his son's garage rafters if it hasn't been thrown away. "Best damn reel ever made." He said the river was deeper then, because of the dams; that you could water ski below South Lebanon. "Try that now and that shallow water above the new bridge will rip your motor right off."

He said when he got older, they caught a lot of bass above Stubbs Mills on C P Swing spinners and pork rinds. And his brother owned a Bass-Oreno, and he remembers wanting one badly. Edgar vividly remembers the river flooding and said you could wade neck deep, "wade where the Smörgåsbord is now." (Duff's Smörgåsbord has been closed for years.) Edgar coughed loudly and seemed tired and I made up an excuse to leave, but Edgar made me promise to return.

"Nobody in this damn place fishes."

Chasing the Snowman
A Short Story set at the Big Rocks

He was an old man and he had never really done anything. Anything that he thought had ever amounted to much anyways, and now he was going fishing. He pulled the old pickup off the two-lane blacktop and onto the berm. Here was a spot just wide enough for the old truck and he had parked here more times than he could count. Across the road a small path led down the bank and over the old railbed to the river. When he was young he used to walk the rails, carefully putting one foot down in front of the other with outstretched arms, like a tightrope walker. He would see how long he could stay up before he had to step off. He remembered how he used to look up the track and see the heat shimmer in waves above the steel and gravel in the summer sun. Waves of heat that made the water of the river seem shockingly cold when later he waded to fish for smallmouth bass. Now the tracks were gone. The steel rails and the ties are all ripped up.

Both his uncles had worked on the railroad, and he remembered how his uncles used to call the ties "sleepers." He said they were called sleepers because it took a whole crew of men to keep them lying in their beds. The earliest dream he could ever remember was a nightmare where all the sleepers woke up and somehow became terrifying monsters. Wooden zombies that chased his young psyche. Now the railbed was covered with blacktop, a new bike and walking trail that ran almost the length of the river. Young families peddling happily past, couples out for a walk, professionals punishing themselves running in expensive jogging suits; many more people got enjoyment from the river now. But part of him missed the railroad, missed the waves of heat rising from the tracks. He climbed heavily out of the cab and gathered his things from the bed of the truck. A white five-gallon bucket containing his fishing gear and bait, an aluminum landing net, and a single fishing rod. It was a very good fishing rod, top of the line seven or eight years ago when he bought it. He owned several fishing rods. All of them were very good. None of them were new.

The old man started down the path, the gravel crunching under the soles of his boots. The path was mostly gravel because of the abandoned railway. Two small gnat-catchers flitted through the bushes around him, buzzing with seemingly more curiosity than anything else. They had always been one of his favorite birds and it was a good omen for the day's fishing. He continued down the hill to the river. That was one of the things he liked about this spot; it was good fishing but had a bank that an old man could still get down.

Soon he came to the river. The path ended on a gravel bar that extended out into the river. To his left the river poured over the end of the gravel bar and ran waist deep and fast for fifty yards before beginning a series of smaller pools and riffles stretching out of sight. Where the river gathered itself before spilling over the bar had always been one of the best smallmouth spots in the river. The old man had spent many summer evenings knee deep in the water casting a small spinner for them. Right at dark he often picked up a sauger here also. It had been a very long time since he had waded out into the fast current here. Some days he still cast a spinner to the good water he could reach from shore.

The water level had just recently gone down, and the old man sat his things down and walked over to a patch of wet sand and mud. It interested him to see who else was about on the river recently. The wet ground was covered in raccoon tracks, and one line of deer tracks heading down to the water. The deer's hooves were splayed wide in the soft ground, and were clearer than usual. From the firm edges and still damp bits of sand kicked up, he judged the track had been made that morning.

Upriver, a heron rose with a loud "kronk" and with heavy wing-beats flew a hundred yards further upstream before landing again. It stepped around nervously for a few seconds then flew upriver out of sight. The old man stopped looking at the rushing water to watch the heron fly, and stared upstream for a long time. Upstream the river was wide and deep, a long curving hole with the outside, and thus deepest part, on the old man's side of the river. Because the outside of the bend, the part that ate away at the bank, was on the old railroad's side of the river, on the old man's side of the river, the railroad had dumped tons of rock and concrete rubble along the bank. Huge slabs of stone and concrete from as small as a washing machine to as big as a small car lay on the bank and out into the water. His dad and uncles always called this hole "the big rocks" for obvious reasons. They had named every hole and riffle in the river and he often thought of making a map with all the names written on it. He knew the names were on the verge of being lost, that in this day of fast cars and highways, none took the time to know one river the way they had known this one.

People loved to talk to him about all he had seen in his lifetime, all the new things that had come along. It's funny, he thought, that all that came to his mind was all the things that had been lost. His grandson could program the DVD player, and, according to his daughter-in-law, was a genius on the computer, but the old man doubted he could even find his way home from here. Actually he had thought VCR instead of DVD player, and had to correct himself. For everything gained there was something lost, the old man was sure of that. He sighed, picked up his bucket and headed up river. A faint path followed the river and wound over and around the huge rocks. The old man walked very slowly, carefully looking before every step. In one spot the path went right up

and over a big slab of concrete and it took him a long time. He stopped when he was back on the ground and leaned back against the stone, his breathing slightly heavy. Up through the trees he could hear a couple kids laughing as they whizzed by on the Scenic Trail. A big carp jumped in the hole and the old man smiled. He didn't believe it had anything to do with the fishing, but he liked it when fish were jumping. Another good omen, he thought.

It took the old man twenty minutes to work his way about a hundred yards upstream from where he first came down to the river. Here a huge slab of concrete lay on its side like a table. An equally large Sycamore hung out over the slab. They had both been there on the riverbank long before he had been coming there, and he had been coming there a long time. A large root of the Sycamore twisted up out of the sandy soil right against the slab, and the old man used this as a step to climb up on the tabletop. There was just enough room for him to sit on the edge with his legs hanging over without touching the water.

He sat down his things and carefully unloaded his bucket and then sat down. Beside him he arranged a small box of hooks, a pair of needle-nose pliers, and his bait jar. On his other side he placed the landing net within easy reach. He rummaged around in his pockets and soon came out with a small Swiss army knife. This knife had a tiny set of scissors and he used these to snip his line loose from where it was tied to the first guide on his rod. Even with knobby fingers drawn up with arthritis, he expertly tied on a small treble hook. He had always been good at doing little things with his fingers, and could still do many things better than most people. He remembered then how his brother used to ask him to tie on lures when they fished together on dark nights. He pulled the knot tight, slowly testing it by grabbing the line a foot or so above the hook, and pulling as hard as he could. Satisfied, he reached for his bait jar. He knew something plastic and less fragile like a Tupperware bowl would have been more practical, but for some reason he was attached to the old jar he kept his bait in. He couldn't remember where he had first gotten it, but he had kept it for years now. It was about the size and shape as a small coffee can, light green glass with a galvanized tin screw top lid. He unscrewed the lid and pinched off a marble-sized piece of bait. He had that morning made a dough of Wheaties, hamburger, and mustard. With that, he had at one time or another managed to catch most of the bottom feeding fish in the river, such as the different kinds of catfish and freshwater drum and carp.

When he was young he had taken some good-natured ribbing from some of his bass and trout fishing buddies for his carp fishing, but he had always felt a fish was a fish. It had always been his philosophy that, all other things being equal, the guy that caught catfish and drum and even bluegills from a place would do better on the flashy gamefish too in the long run. Upstream from where he sat was the deepest, slowest part of the entire hole. He sat watching this deep water as he molded the doughball onto his hook. About twenty yards away the current curled back on itself along the bank and almost stopped. There he cast his doughball.

The old man carefully laid the rod beside him on the concrete slab. He flipped the bail so a big fish could take line without pulling in his rod. He pulled a quarter out of his pocket and laid it on top of the loose line, to keep it from pulling off the reel in the slight current of the hole. The old man breathed deeply, the wet musky smell of the river and the mud making him smile. He looked up at the blue sky watching the warm breeze sway the tops of the trees, now bursting with tiny new leaves.

When he looked down the line was no longer under the quarter and a great deal of it was rushing away downriver. He carefully picked up the rod, spinning the handle to engage the bail and set the hook. The rod bounced up and down in place and then the line rushed out even faster than before. The old man held the rod high, letting the bend in the rod cushion the line, and soon the fish turned planing diagonally across the river. A couple more minutes, and a big carp was lying, half on its side, finning in the water at the old man's feet.

He carefully and slowly reached over and found the landing net by feel, never taking his eyes off the fish. He slowly lowered the net in the water and then leaned forward and scooped up the fish. Or tried to--as the net went under the fish, it suddenly came back to life and shot out into the river, line screaming off the reel. Three more minutes and he scooped

again, this time netting the fish.

The fish was heavy for the old man as he swung it up onto the flat stone. It flopped wildly, and it took the old man a little too long to unhook it and return it to the river. It just sort of lay there working its gills and fins for a moment, before scooting out of sight into deeper water.

The old man was tired but happy as he slowly re-baited and cast again. He leaned back on one elbow enjoying the sunshine and his thoughts wandered back once again to the long gone railroad. When he was a younger man he often became restless and spent many days just walking the tracks for miles. He remembered how one winter it had been bitter cold with snow and ice for a couple weeks, and then the weather broke warm and sunny. That day he set off down the tracks and found a trail of footprints made out of ice and snow on the bare wet ground and ties. Sometime in the past week, someone had walked that way and compacted the snow almost into ice so that when things warmed all that remained were their footprints. At least that's what logic told him. His heart saw them as some special magical tracks of a snowman getting the hell out of there as it warmed.

He followed the snow tracks for miles but finally turned back knowing he would be walking in the dark before he made it home. In the evening sun he then saw now all the tracks of snow he had followed all day were gone in the evening sun.

The warm spring sun made the old man sleepy, and his last thoughts were of the snowman tracks and how he hadn't thought of them in years.

Some time later the line slipped once more from under the quarter and zipped off unnoticed. The line caught on the bail and the rod pulled off the rock landing in the river with a small plop.

The old man never stirred, there in the warm spring sunshine.

A State Record Swimming in the Little Miami River?

So I was back at the hole where the week before I'd caught a 19-inch-plus smallmouth. But a cold front had blown through and the smallies had kicked the proverbial bucket. In the last couple days I'd caught nothing but small bass and not a lot of them.

But I'd caught the only decent fish, that 19-inch smallie, a week ago in the tail of the pool. Every year I catch big smallies up in the head of the pool, but never down in the tail. It was a couple hours before dark, so I decided to take my time and fish the entire length of the hole. I think what makes this such a good place is that the entire length of the hole has a rock bottom, with almost no silt at all. The river's low right now, so I tied on a small square billed bomber alphabet plug. Silver with a back and purplish cast to it. The first cast or two were right in the slick where the water speeds up before spilling over the riffle. Then I cast a bit further up. Still close to the riffle, but in deeper, say waist deep water. Thump. Something big hit the crank. But it just bored slowly upstream slowly pulling drag. I just assumed it was a catfish. Then it turned and ran back downstream again, slowly, but you could tell it was a heavy fish. And so it went for a minute or two as I gained a bit of line each time. Finally it rolled and I saw golden brown and thought "Oh Wow! It's a big saugeye."

I beached it and had it just about unhooked before I realized it didn't have marks to tell it was a saugeye. There was not the big spot at the base of the dorsal that saugeye and walleyes have. And there was not the white on the anal fin or tail like saugeye has.

"Jeepers, this thing is a sauger! I didn't think they made them that big!"

I looked it over as carefully as I could and couldn't make anything out of it but a sauger. I measured the fish carefully; it taped out right at 25 inches. The thing fought better on land than in the water and I'd already dropped it once. I snapped a quick picture of myself and the fish, then held it in the water for a minute or two before snapping a couple more. I was worried about the fish making it at this point, and didn't take enough pictures of its fins to satisfy everyone that it was a sauger. I've caught some grief over that. I then held it by the tail and worked it back and forth in the water, until it was stable and strong enough to swim away under its own power.

When I posted the fish on the Ohio game fishing forum the majority of people thought it was a sauger, but a few doubted my ID. Too big; it's gotta be a saugeye. Even though you can plainly see in every picture there's no white on the fins. But in every picture, its dorsal is folded down. I really don't care about that, though, I know what I caught. If I were in it for bragging rights, the fish would be dead and in the freezer right now. But come January I'll know the state record is swimming in the LMR. You see, the current record is 24.5 inches, a half inch shorter than this fish. My fish wouldn't have broken the record today, though. That other fish was caught in late winter and weighed 7.31 pounds full of eggs. But, but come January my fish will still be alive and full of eggs of its own.

The Big One That Got Away

A whole day free. The wife had to work; no baby-sitting chores; I knew exactly where I wanted to spend it. There's this hole, you see, where the river makes a sharp turn digging a nice hole then a riffle and a long slow hole. It's one of the most consistent fish producing spots I know. You can almost count on catching at least a half dozen bass every time you go there. I'd even caught a couple big catfish there on lures while bass fishing. The hole has one more thing going for it, it's really not that easy to get to. You have to walk a hundred fifty yards down a dry creek bed, then the hole fishes best from the far side so you wade across the river above to do it right. I've

never seen anyone else fishing there during the day, much less at night, so that's where I headed.

I got there early afternoon and took my time, gathered enough firewood for a nice fire and set up a nice little base camp. I'd packed in a few special things too. A couple empty two-liter pop bottles, some strong nylon rope, and a handful of big 5/0 hooks. The makings of a trot line. Plus the two big bait-casting rods. You know the ones with the clickers and star drags, big enough to handle the fish you dream of catching, not the ones you actually do catch.

I then went to work, fishing worms on my light spinning rod, and soon had a couple drum and a pumpkinseed for bait. I tied each two liter bottle to heavy rocks with enough slack to let them float about chest deep and sunk them about 40 yards apart just below the rock bar where the hole first gets deep. Then I stretched nylon cord between the two bottles with a half dozen of the big 5/0 hooks on droppers spaced out evenly. I baited these with cut pieces of drum and the pumpkinseed, and as a finishing touch, blew up and tied two balloons as floats along the main line. It was beautiful. I was sure I would catch a giant. With a couple hours left till dark, I then hid the two bait-casters in the bushes and began lure fishing upstream through the faster water with my spinning rod.

The bass fishing was fabulous and by dark I'd probably landed a dozen bass with a couple more drum on a smoke metalflake grub. I then built a fire, changed into dry shoes, put on a flannel shirt and threw out the bait-casting rods to wait on a big catfish. The word wait should probably be followed by a couple lines that are just blank to convey more of the meaning of the word, as the wait for a big catfish to bite can sometimes be epic. Every half hour or so another drum would hit just to keep things interesting. Plus two softshell turtles, one small and cute and one big enough to make me be extra careful not to get within range of that beak-like mouth.

Some time in the middle of the night, I heard a tremendous splashing in the direction of the trotline. Grabbing the flashlight I got there just in time to see a very big fish roll once on the dropper baited with the pumpkinseed.

Then before I could wade in to land it, the line went quiet – too quiet. The big cat had come loose, and gotten off. I had two nice runs on the rods, but came up empty, with the bait gone. So I put on a night-crawler, trying to catch some smaller drum for bait. After a few minutes , the line tore off in a rush, and I was fast into a nice carp. But no catfish.

On both sides of me, owls cried during the night. First the eerie unworldly cries of a screech owl, then the familiar cry of a barred owl. I hooted back at the barred owl and he flew closer, calling out off and on all during the night. At dawn, the score was ten drum, one carp, one small gar, and a grand total of zero catfish.

I moved up above the riffle to the smaller hold above. Instantly a drum was on, and they bit as fast as I could re-bait for about an hour. I even managed to catch a decent smallmouth on the nightcrawler fished on the bottom. I think I was even more surprised than he was.

Finally, I went back down river, took up the trot line, gathered my things, and waded the river and headed up to the creek that was my way out. Just then a great fish broke water upstream of me, not in the way that big carp breach, but in a huge tail-slapping roll. It looked gigantic. Sneaking slowly up the bank, I crept up behind a weed bed and peak-ed over the bank. In the shallows were eight or ten big fish. "Carp", I thought, but they didn't look just right. Carp in the river are a graceful, streamlined fish, and these were stockier rounder fish. I watched for a bit then it hit me. Buffalo!

The world record Buffalo is 88 pounds, though commercial fishermen have caught much larger ones. I think the Ohio record is under fifty pounds. In this pod of fish, there were two that were very big. I'd never caught a big one, and am no person to judge their size, but the largest looked a bit shorter than the 37 pound carp I'd caught earlier in the year, and at least as broad across the back. Since Buffalo are a rounder, deeper-bellied fish, this was a very big fish.

The water was shallow and clear. The fish would spook if I made much commotion at all, so I hooked on a nightcrawler on an un-weighted hook, and crept forward behind the tall weeds. After a minute or two one of the big fish, and a smaller one swam my way. I cast the worm out ahead of them and waited. They both swam right over the bait and the line twitched and began to move. I set the hook and was fast into a fish--the smaller one of course. Not that he was small. I guess around ten pounds, but by the time I landed him in the shallow water, every fish had left the pool.

All in all a very fine fishing trip.

The Sound of a Train Not Running

The Peace of Wild Things

When despair for the world grows in me
and I wake in the night at the least sound
in fear of what my life and my children's lives may be,
I go and lie down where the wood drake
rests in his beauty on the water, and the great heron feeds.
I come into the peace of wild things
who do not tax their lives with forethought
of grief. I come into the presence of still water.
And I feel above me the day-blind stars
waiting with their light. For a time
I rest in the grace of the world, and am free.

by Wendell Berry

Another long day at work. Too long but at least with a glimmer of light at the end of the tunnel. For tonight the schedule was gloriously free. Warm, muggy, it felt more like one of the first days of summer rather than one of the last days of spring. In the pack I threw the first things I could come up with, a peanut butter sandwich and a pop top can of pineapples, some water and ran for the door. Twenty minutes later I'm parked at the Fork. Todd's Fork? Anderson Fork? Flat Fork? East Fork? North Fork? There's a dozen "forks" on the Little Miami, and that's as close as I'm coming to saying where I was. Some will recognize it from the pictures. Please don't tell the whole world about it. You cross the Fork on a two-lane blacktop, then park on the otherside next to an old railroad overpass. All that remains is the two stone structures made with a craftsmanship that insures they will be there long after I'm gone. The old railbed is just a gravely hump overgrown into a thicket cutting across a big bend in the fork to hit it again a mile upstream. A small path cuts down the bank beside the road bridge to the water's edge.

Here I waded in. The fishing's no good, but it's easier walking up the streambed than on the banks. Upstream in the bend is deeper water but the sun was still hot. A fish halfheartedly slashed at my Rebel minnow but I didn't hook it. A great blue heron lifted off with a "Kronk" and flew upstream. I'd flush it twice more before it had enough and left. There was a small island held in place mostly by the gnarled roots of an old Sycamore. I love the old trees, and never tire of looking at the twisted puzzles made by the contorted, tortile roots. It was shallow on each side of the little island but just upstream everything came back together in a deep riffle pouring out of a long hole. A big turtle plopped off a log into some slack water on the left side.

Way upstream I heard the manic laughter of a kingfisher as it swooped down from an overhanging Sycamore branch to grab a minnow. This long hole has several of these long branches overhanging the stream. Besides being the perfect perch for a hunting kingfisher they were the kind of place my grandfather used to look for to hang a "jingle line" for catfish. Fishing with jingle lines seems a lost art. You hang a baitfish on a stout line and a big hook from a long springy branch so the bait would struggle just under the surface. On a still summer night it's sometimes deadly on good-sized catfish.

I caught a couple small smallmouth bass from the riffle on an inline spinner then tied back on my Rebel minnow. Throwing over into the slack water by the turtle's log, I twitched the lure once. Splash, a nice strike. It turned out to be a nice spotted bass, maybe 13 or 14 inches long.

After admiring the fish I began to wade up the hole. It was a long flat-bottomed hole, anywhere from waist deep to mid thigh. The best fish I caught out of the next hundred yards was a big rock bass that hammered the minnow plug by a jumble of woody debris.

Now, in the distance I could see my destination, the old railroad bridge crossing the stream. The bridge crossed on two high banks and was maybe forty feet above the fork. I don't know if I'd have liked walking it when new, but that was out of the question now. About halfway through, most of the crucial cross ties were missing. It was a beautiful old bridge. More beautiful than useful. Underneath one side was a small sandbar, while on the other, the stream, blocked by the stone structure that had dug a deep hole. Deep and full of possibility.

On the sandbar another old Sycamore leaned back away from the stream, its trunk creating a perfect backrest with a soft sandy seat. I sat there a long time eating my sandwich and draining my can of pineapple. I noticed several swallows flitting in and out of crevices on the stone bridge abutments. In a tree next to me, a robin eyed me nervously with a worm dangling from its beak for its hungry chicks somewhere nearby. I read somewhere that the average robin family eats something in the neighborhood of 14 feet of worms a day. That's a lot of work.

It was still early, and I leaned back against my tree and closed my eyes. When I opened them again it was much later. Long shadows hung over the water. I sat there awhile, watching the swallows swoop over the pool and flit in and out of their holes, no doubt also feeding hungry little ones too. Finally I got up and tied on a jig, and fished the deep water. I caught two small fish about ten inches long and another maybe seven inches long upstream. Then in the next riffle I caught three, from 10 to 14 inches long.

Now it was getting late, and the frogs' trilling filled the calm air. I pulled a sweatshirt out of my pack and slipped it on. I switched spools on my reel. From light six pound test to heavy braid. I tied on a lipless crankbait, and waded back down to the deep hole by the bridge. Nothing hit. Overhead the last of the swallows were replaced by the flittering of bats as they worked upstream and down in big ovals hunting insects. I probably stayed too long, but the scene was so peaceful the last thing I wanted to do was go.

Then, in the middle of a cast I was no longer paying much attention to, the line stopped dead. Then it moved off slowly upstream, the rod bending double.

The fish bore upstream, almost out of the hole, then slowly swam back downstream past me. I followed. Several minutes later, and quite a bit down the long flat hole I finally beached the big shovelhead on a small gravel bank. I snapped a few photos then held it upright for a moment by the tail till it could swim off again. I waded back downstream towards the truck. I turned on my headlamp but found I could see better without it and switched it off again, wading slowly into the coming night. Finally back at the truck, I heard the hooting of a barred owl way back upstream as I climbed in and headed regretfully back to the world of people.

The Big One ...

So I left work Thursday night for a long weekend of bow hunting, with a bit of fishing thrown in. Little did I know it would end up a fishing trip, with a bit of hunting thrown in.

Saturday was the first day of bow hunting season for deer. So Friday I stopped by Scioto Brush Creek for three hours of fishing, before heading out to my hunting cabin. Well Scioto Brush Creek looked nothing at all like our streams, you would think it hadn't rained there for months. Crystal clear. It's a stream not at all wader friendly even though it's not big. Not a lot of places to get on the stream either. I hit it just below the covered bridge at Otway. I caught about a dozen smallies in no time though. I imagine that if you put in a canoe this would be the perfect smallie stream, miles and miles of stream all to yourself, all running through beautiful woods and farm country.

The next morning I was up the tree about one hour before arrowing a big doe. So after taking care of the deer, my hunting trip turned into a fishing trip. That night sitting around the campfire I looked up to see a beautiful ring around the moon.

The next morning, it was back to Scioto Brush Creek. This time I fished longer and must have caught thirty smallmouth all in the 8 to 14 inch range. Plus some gorgeous longeared sunfish that look like jewels.

Then another night of staring at the night sky and the campfire. The next day the forecast was for rain so I started back towards home, and the Little Miami. Right away I caught a really nice smallmouth on a spinner.

There was another guy there fishing, so I walked down and asked him to snap a photo. As he's taking the photo he says, "Hey I know you... You're the guy on the Ohio Game-fishing forum that caught the giant goldfish." Yep, that's me, the giant goldfish guy. Nope, not the guy that's got thirty deer with a bow or has two ten pound bass on the wall...nope, I'm the giant goldfish guy. Every time, I'm the giant goldfish guy. Thanks.

It rained a bit as I worked my way up to the same riffle where I had caught the nice smallie earlier. In ten minutes I caught three smallies that probably averaged 15 inches, and lost another, so I knew tonight was going to be something special. In the calm water across the river I kept seeing bass running minnows right up on the bank and a couple times bust one on the surface so I switched to a pop-r. On the second cast a big fish nailed it. It jumped twice and then I could just see it open its mouth underwater and blow out the plug. I was shaking, as it was easily the biggest smallie I'd had on all year.

I then decided you only get a chance or two like this all year, so I'm fishing till dark or a big fish, whichever comes first. I caught two nice smallies in the hole down below on a crankbait. Then a little bass on a spinner on the riffle below that. It was getting darker and raining a bit harder as I headed back up to the spot. Nothing there. I again switched lures. Nothing. Then the pop-r back on, nope.

I put the grub back on and hooked a Buffalo. It was around ten pounds, and I loosened the drag way up since it was six pound test line I had on. After babying the fish around forever, it came off right as I was going to land it.

I threw right back in the same spot, and "wham!", the rod bent double. I thought, well I'm not going to baby this one since I lost the last one anyways. As I leaned back on the rod a big smallie catapulted skyward! After a few very nervous moments I finally lipped this one without her getting off. After snapping a few photos I measured her carefully. She was 5/8ths past the 20" mark. It's funny but if I had actually landed the Buffalo, I'm not sure I wouldn't have packed it in and headed home right then.

Snapshots of Friends

Here are some pictures of some of our favorite plants, bugs, insects, critters and beasts that call the Little Miami River Watershed home. Some of the pictures were taken by me on trips to the LMR. Others were contributed, courtesy of Jerry Snider, Ron Levi, Bill Schroeder, and the Ohio Department of Natural Resources.

GREAT BLUE HERON

The Little Miami River Valley is one of the best spots for viewing this amazing bird. Several breeding colonies exist along the river and its tributaries. In Summer, it seems every hole you come to holds a heron or two that spook at your approach. An excellent predator, the heron stands stock still till a small fish or frog comes along, then the long neck shoots out spearing its prey with its long sharp beak, as shown in these pictures. Large and well-equipped to defend themselves, herons in one rookery along the Little Miami even shared a big Sycamore tree with an eagle. The eagle took over the large nest of one heron to raise its young. All the others stayed, sharing the tree with the imposing raptor.

THE BALD EAGLE

Finally off the endangered species list, the bald eagle has actually now started nesting on the Little Miami. The bald eagle is also often spotted on the big reservoirs of the Little Miami watershed such as Caesar Creek and East Fork as well as at the many gravel pits in the floodplain.

Eagles and their cousins, the Osprey, are true river success stories. No matter how many times I spot one while fishing the river, it never fails to thrill. In November, (so I wouldn't disturb the residents) I poked around for a while under an eagle's nest in a big Sycamore just off the river. There were unidentified small bones, pieces of three or four turtle shells, some fur, and three or four eagle feathers, which now grace the desk I'm writing this on.

MOREL MUSHROOM

LONGEAR SUNFISH

Every now and then when cutting across some river bottom in spring, I'll spot a morel mushroom poking up through the leaf litter. Time to drop everything and devote the rest of the day to hunting for more. I know dedicated mushroom hunters have all kinds of signs to tell them when to mushroom hunt but it varies with every spot depending on how the sun, shade, moisture, and Lord only knows what that's a bit different in each spot. These signs and notions of when to hunt are called "SWATS"(Scientific Wild Ass Theories) . I do know nothing's better when coated with egg, rolled in flour and fried. The actual mushroom above ground is just the tip of the iceberg, just the fruiting body that puts out spores.

Most mushrooms spreading out through the soil and leaves can live for years, so a spot you've found them in before is worth checking out every year. When reading about morels I found there was disagreement on how many types there are. Wikipedia says there are anywhere from 5 or 6 to 50 (!) though most mushroom hunters just say the yellow, white, or black ones. There are, as everyone knows, poisonous mushrooms out there, but morels are pretty easy to identify, and anyone with a decent guidebook should be safe gathering this prize of gourmet cooks everywhere.

This gorgeous little fish is the most common sunfish in the Little Miami. In Ohio's ponds and lakes you will find the nearly identical pumpkinseed (which doesn't have the gill flap of the longear), though both are called pumpkinseeds in the local fishing lingo. In quiet backwaters or big eddies the longear readily bops a dry fly or sponge spider and makes for great fly rod fun. Hardy longears are also often caught and used for shovelhead bait.

Longears spawn multiple times once the water temperature reaches the low 70s between mid-May and mid-August. A single large female can lay over 22,000 eggs, a strategy that works well when everything in the river thinks you are delicious. The world record is under two pounds, but longears make up for a lack of size by scrappiness. The Outdoor Writers of Ohio lists the Ohio record at only 0.41 pounds so this might be one of the more breakable records out there.

TRILLIUMS

Trilliums are perennials that sprout each season from small irregularly shaped bulbs called rhizomes. Like all spring woodland flowers, their early growth takes advantage of spring's sunshine before the trees leaf out. The early pioneers and native Americans thought that potions made out of trilliums were aids in pregnancy and childbirth and were also supposedly key ingredients in love potions. The trillium was also used as food by the Native Americans and the early pioneers. Trillium is an example of a plant whose seeds are spread by ants. Trillium seeds have a fleshy organ called an elaiosome that attracts ants. The ants take the seeds to their nest, where they eat the elaiosomes and put the seeds in their mound's garbage dump, where they are protected until they germinate. This is called myrmecochory, or ant-mediated dispersal. Trilliums are a common wildflower of the woods all along the Little Miami but are especially plentiful in the big woods around Oregonia.

JACK IN THE PULPIT

The Jack in the pulpit has always fascinated me. From its strange flower to the burning calcium oxalate crystals present in the plant, everything about this wildflower is just a bit weird. Adding to the weirdness is the plant's ability to produce female flowers one year and male flowers the next. The how and why of this is not completely understood but seems to depend on how many resources the plant has available to it that particular year since it takes much more to produce seeds as a female plant. The plant contains calcium oxalate crystals which cause a very powerful burning sensation when eaten. This burning goes away when the bulb is dried and they were gathered for food by Native Americans. This otherwise powerful protection doesn't seem to help with birds though as I once killed a big tom turkey stuffed full of Jacks. The strange flower of the Jack in the pulpit can vary quite a bit in color from a light green to being heavily striped with purple. These flowers do not attract butterflies or other insects with a sweet nectar but instead are pollinated by flies attracted by an odd smell. A preparation of the root was reported to have been used by Native

Americans as a treatment for sore eyes. Preparations were also made to treat rheumatism, snakebites, and bronchitis. Jacks can live to be from 20 to 100 years old and are common in the larger woods all along the Little Miami valley. All-in-all, a very strange little plant indeed.

SQUAWROOT

MAIDENHAIR FERN

Another strange plant of the Little Miami's woodlands is Squawroot or bear corn. This odd little plant looks like a cross between a pine cone and a mushroom but in reality it is a small perennial parasitic plant. Squawroot is parasitic on the roots of woody plants, especially oaks and beech, and is more common higher on the ridges lining the river than down in the floodplain. The plant gets it's name bear corn from being gathered by black bears in springtime before a lot of green foods are available. The name Squawroot is attributed to its being used by Native American as a treatment to relieve the symptoms of menopause. Later in summer the plant turns browner and becomes tougher and dried out. Squawroot does not have chlorophyll and is unable to engage in photosynthesis. This is called achlorophyllous.

Maidenhair fern was used by Native Americans for a lot of medicinal potions for everything from cough medicine to keeping hair shiny and healthy. The Cherokee had a legend that if a maiden handles a stem and the lacy leaves do not flicker, her virtue is assured! It was also thought that the ferns could help prevent baldness when used in herbal remedies. Sadly this fern has never been proven to work in either case.

Maidenhair fern likes rich woodlands and thrives in the bigger woods along the middle Little Miami river valley because of its rich limestone soil. Never common anywhere, finding a patch of these lovely ferns is always a treat.

MUSKRAT

One of the most common mammals along the river, muskrats get their name from the two scent glands which are found near their tail which give off a strong "musky" odor which the muskrat uses to mark its territory. Muskrats in the Little Miami den mostly in the bank, but in marshy areas such as Spring Valley Wildlife Area, they build houses out of cattails and mud. They feed on cattails and other aquatic vegetation as well as the occasional mussel. Their fur is prized for its warmth and was sometimes trimmed and dyed and called "Hudson seal" fur. The muskrats fur contains natural oils that repel water and is the key ingredient in the floating fly pattern called the Adams, the most widely used dry fly in the world. Muskrats serve as food for mink, foxes, coyotes, eagles, snakes, large owls, hawks, otters, snapping turtles, and large fish such as muskie.   Fortunately, in the Little Miami they make up for this by breeding like rabbits. In more than one Native American creation myth it is the muskrat who dives to the bottom of the primordial sea to bring up mud from which the earth was created. Muskrat was used for food by early explorers and pioneers. The Roman Catholic Archdiocese of Detroit created a dispensation allowing Catholics to consume muskrat on Ash Wednesday and the Fridays of Lent. Because the muskrat lives in water, it was considered equivalent to fish. Muskrats are most active at night or near dawn and dusk and can often be seen swimming in the Little Miami at those times.

DRAGONFLIES AND DAMSELFLIES

Dragonfly and damselfly nymphs are especially important in the rivers food chain where they act as fierce predators of small insects and then in turn are eaten with relish by many fish species. In some larger species the nymphal stage can last for up to five years, but most species carry out their life cycle in one year. Damselfly adults fly slower than dragonflies which are the true speedsters of the river's insect world. Dragonflies can fly forward at about 100 body-lengths per second, and even backwards at about 3 body-lengths per second! Though dragonflies are predators, they themselves are eaten by many predators. Birds, spiders, fish, water bugs, lizards, frogs, and even other large dragonflies have all been seen eating damsel and dragonflies. But the dragonflies speed and agility in flight make them a hard catch. Plus of course their excellent eyesight, dragonfly eyes contain up to 30,000 individual lenses which all seem to find me whenever I try to get close enough to one for a photograph.

MAYAPPLE

Mayapple contains quercetin, kaempferol, podophyllin, isorhamnetin, gallic-acid, berberine, alpha-peltatin, chemicals that are being studied for their healing, anticancer and other properties. These compounds make the mayapple poisonous in all parts except the ripe fruit which can be eaten. It really doesn't taste very good, though. Trust me I've tried some.

The top and root produce nausea and vomiting, and even inflammation of the stomach and intestines, which has been known to prove fatal. In moderate doses, it is a drastic purgative. In other words, don't eat it!

Mayapple was once called the "witche's umbrella" and thought to be employed by them as a poison. In Europe its close relative is called mandrake and was believed in folklore to be alive. Its screams when pulled from the ground reportedly would render a man permanently insane. What mayapple is besides all this is a pretty little plant common to moist woodland all up and down the Little Miami Valley.

GOLDENSEAL

Goldenseal is often used as a multi-purpose remedy, and is thought by many herbalists to possess many medicinal properties. Besides being a topical antimicrobial, it is also taken as a digestion aid, and supposedly removes canker sores when gargled. I have used goldenseal by boiling the root in water and applying the liquid to an itchy and inflamed eye. I thought it helped, but I'm not endorsing its use so don't sue me if you use it. I'm just saying I tried it, that's all, okay?

Goldenseal may be purchased in salve, tablet, tincture form, or as a bulk powder. Goldenseal is often used to boost the medicinal effects of other herbs it is blended or formulated with. Goldenseal roots can be dug and dried and sold by the pound but for just a few dollars per pound. I'd think it would be hard work to average minimum wage doing this.

BANEBERRY

Old time ginseng hunters used the presence of baneberry as an indicator of woodland suitable for ginseng. With ginseng becoming very rare in the Little Miami woods, baneberry is still worthy of attention for its own sinister reasons. Baneberry contains cardiogenic toxins than can have an immediate sedative effect on human cardiac muscle tissue. These toxins are present in the plant's lovely berries and children should be watched around the tempting berries. These berries also give the plant its other common name, "Doll's Eyes."

SNAKES ALONG THE RIVER

There are roughly eight or ten species of snake you might expect to find along the Little Miami. None are poisonous, though Spring Valley Wildlife Area is home to a few Massasauga rattlesnakes (whose venom can be toxic) in its marshes which border the river. Even there, you probably have a better chance of winning the lottery than encountering this endangered snake. When you encounter a snake along the river it's probably one of the two snakes; either the common garter snake and the northern water snake. If someone tells you they saw a water moccasin in the river, they have more than likely seen a northern water snake which is common all up and down the river.

RACCOON

Unless you venture out right after a rain it's hard to find a patch of mud along the river that does not contain raccoon tracks. This adaptable mammal thrives seemingly everywhere and forages up and down the riverbank for crayfish, small fish, garbage from houses, and vegetables from farms and gardens. Although they look cute and cuddly, they are as tough as nails and I have seen them run grey fox off a food source. Heaven help the small dog that corners one and starts a fight.

During the daytime, raccoons sleep in hollow trees or logs and other animals' abandoned dens. They are nocturnal and are often seen right at dark or by night fishermen on the river. Even though the raccoon does not really hibernate it lays up in its den for weeks during the cold winter.

Long prolonged periods of bad weather in winter can be hard on raccoon. They counter this by storing large amounts of fat, which add to their cute roly-poly looks. During late summer nights spent trying to catch a catfish on the river, I've seen raccoons foraging in the moonlight on the opposite bank and every time they remind me somehow of rowdy youngsters, young Tom Sawyers and Huck Finns wandering from adventure to adventure.

WILD TURKEY

Like the whitetail deer, in my youth there were no wild turkey at all in the Little Miami watershed. Nowadays I pass a field on my way to work that in late winter holds fifty or sixty of these great birds every day. By 1904 the last wild turkey was gone from Ohio. The bird was reintroduced in the fifties and in 1966, only nine counties were opened for gobbler hunting. During that first season, 12 birds were checked in. Most years now over 20,000 gobblers are tagged. The numbers in Ohio reflect a trend nationwide. Wild turkeys were hunted nearly to extinction nationwide in the 1930s. Now, there are over 8 million living in the United States.

RAMPS

Ramps or wild leeks are, next to a good venison steak, my favorite wild food. Every spring I head out with a lunch and water bottle stuck in a backpack determined to return with the pack filled with ramps. Most people eat only the onion like bulb but I gather the tops as well. Dehydrated, they make their most wonderful spice all.

I grill nothing without sprinkling a pinch of dried ramps on first. And baked potatoes are never better than when slathered with butter and a pinch of ramps. The bulbs can also be dehydrated and later added to soups and chili. But the way I like the bulbs best is fresh and fried with potatoes. The strong garlic flavor is something you either love or hate.

Ramps can be found in rich damp hollows of the bigger woods along the river in spring but as smmer starts, like many woodland plants the tops dry up and die back.

GREY FOX

The thickets and woodlands bordering the river are more often the home of the grey fox than it's more famous brother, the red fox. While the red fox loves nothing more than the open fields and pastures away from the riverbank, the grey fox is right at home along the river. The gray fox's ability to climb trees is shared only with the Asian raccoon dog among canids. Its strong, hooked claws allow it to scramble up trees to escape predators such as the coyote, or to reach food sources. The grey fox is omnivorous and eats everything from rabbits and mice to wild grapes, and the myriad of small creatures that abound along the river.

WHITE TAIL DEER

When I was young there were almost no deer at all in the Little Miami watershed. Now they are among its most common residents, a huge success story for conservation. In the quiet of the evening, when the canoes have stopped coming and the river is silent except for the sound of water, in secluded spots you're almost certain to see wary whitetails slip down to the river for a drink. Or see a big doe cross the river in a riffle way upstream or crash off as you walk out in the darkness. Among the most beautiful creatures on earth, deer now grace the river valley in numbers approaching those present before the first settlers.

CANADA GOOSE

Before 1950, Canada geese were only known as migrants in Ohio. In the 1950s, the Ohio Division of Wildlife initiated a program to establish resident flocks within the state and the rest, as they say, is history. Seemingly every pond and puddle and stream holds a few geese and they nest all up and down the Little Miami. Indeed they have done so well my father has taken to calling them "sky carp." Still a flock flying in a vee across an early morning sky is as beautiful as ever.

CICADA

In 2008 my wife and I attended the big pow-wow held every year at Fort Ancient. That year the sounds of the drummers and singers were almost drowned out by another chorus for the big woods surrounding the mounds and walls held countless millions of periodical cicadas. Studies have found densities as high as 1.5 million cicadas per acre and there's a lot of acreage along the river here. At the base of big trees we found hundreds of empty nymph cases of hatched cicadas under each tree.

There are several broods in the hundred-mile river valley and they do not all hatch the same year. One brood hatched in the upper watershed four years before these Fort Ancient cicadas. After an emergence, it's seventeen years before another outbreak, so you're not going to see many of these wonders of nature in your lifetime.

The abundance of cicadas during an emergence is not uniform. Some local areas in the Little Miami Valley have great numbers, while others only a few miles away may have very few. Collectively these cicadas stage one of the greatest spectacles that can be witnessed anywhere in the natural world. The emergence of periodical cicadas has an immense effect on the forest ecosystem. Just as they all emerge at once, all these bugs all die in just a few weeks of each other. The death of so many cicadas coming all at once gives a sudden burst of fertilizer to the woodlands and cicadas falling in the water are gobbled up by hungry fish. Almost all the mammals in the woods feed on cicadas in a breakout year. I've read they even become a favorite food of animals we think of as strictly vegetarian such as squirrels at such times and bird numbers also increase as thousands of birds move in to feast on the bounty. For just a month or two every seventeen years, every-thing changes and makes us realize again what a different world can exist all around us.

TURTLES, FROGS AND TOADS

The classic reptile of the woodlands around the river is the box turtle. The box turtle gets its name from its centrally-hinged lower shell which enables both the front and rear parts of the shell to be drawn up tight against the upper shell. Long lived, their biggest danger comes from cars. The bigger woods around Fort Ancient and Oregonia seem to me to hold the greatest numbers of these gentle turtles. Opposite in temperament are the softshell and snapping turtles that inhabit the river, striking out with lightning speed at a fisherman who manages to hook one. But the most famous turtle in the river has to be the painted turtle.

They are very fond of basking in the sun and can be seen by the dozens on logs and along the banks of the Little Miami, plopping off into the river at the approach of a canoe or fisherman. Ohio is home to 15 species of frogs and toads, and I cannot pretend to know them all. There are a few, though, known to everyone who pokes around the river. Looking like a small bullfrog, the northern green frog can be distinguished by the lines of folded skin running down its sides. Like any good frog worthy of its name, the northern green frog eats just about anything it can fit in its mouth and is an important part of the river's food chain.

The much larger bullfrog is a monster haunting all the small creatures of the riverbank. With their huge gaping mouths, bullfrogs have been known to eat everything from bugs and smaller frogs to small birds and snakes. I remember fishing a buzzbait up along the bank in the middle of the night hoping for a big bass, and catching a big bullfrog that attacked the big lure.

The American toad is nocturnal and can be found throughout the watershed anywhere from urban yards to woodlands. The 2- or 3-inch long amphibian comes in a variety of colors, but is most commonly brown. There are dark blotches all over its body. Inside these blotches are 1 or 2 "warts" These warts are actually glands that produce a nasty tasting liquid, protecting them from predators. The toad is a great predator of insects and the average toad will eat up to 3,000 insects a month. The toad does not drink water, but absorbs it through its skin.

BEAVER

North America's largest rodent, the beaver is now thriving up and down the Little Miami and it's tributaries. The beaver does not build it's famous dams in the river but instead dens in the bank. On almost every fishing trip or walk along the riverbank you will find sign of beaver in the floodplain along the river.

BLOODROOT

Bloodroot blooms before almost anything else along the river, with blooms opening even before the leaves completely unfurl. Bloodroot, like Jack in the pulpit, is one of those plants whose seeds are spread by ants, a process called myrmecochory. The ants take the seeds to their nest where they eat the fleshy part and put the seeds in their nest debris, where they are protected until they germinate. Bloodroot was used as a dye by early pioneers and as a remedy for warts. Bloodroot is also being studied as a possible treatment for oral cancers but the U.S. Food and Drug Administration has listed some of these products among its "187 Fake Cancer 'Cures' Consumers Should Avoid."

OTTER

In the last few years a new predator has returned to the Little Miami after long absence, the wonderful otter. I'll never forget my wife and I standing high on a riverbank watching a family group frolic in the shallows. Otter seem to just enjoy life and even the adults spend a lot of time at play. In 1986 the Ohio Division of Wildlife began to re-introduce the otter to the state. Since then they have spread over two thirds of the state.

BLUE SUCKER

The Blue Sucker is one of several species found in the Little Miami River that is regarded as "threatened" by Ohio DNR. They are so named because of their slate-blue appearance. First discovered in 1817, blue suckers have since been reported from the Missouri, Mississippi, Ohio and Rio Grande Rivers and most major tributaries. Generally, they are found to prefer living in large rivers with strong currents and high turbid-
ity. Pictured below is a picture of a blue sucker collected and carefully released by Ohio DNR personnel during a fish count near Milford. Anyone catch-

ing one of these rare beauties should treat it with great care, making sure it is released and returned to the LMR in good condition.

MOUNTAIN MADTOM AND NORTHERN MADTOM

Who could not be curious about a fish with such a quaint name? Their real scientific names are no-turus eleutherus, and noturus stigmosus. There are two very good reasons not to fool with them if you are lucky enough to catch or net one. First, they are both listed as endangered species in Ohio. Second, they are among those species of catfish that have venom in their dorsal fin. If you step on one without shoes, or handle one carelessly you are likely to get a very painful poke or sting that you will not soon forget. Adults are 3-5 inches long, so it is possible to catch one on a hook. If you do, please handle with care and release immediately for your sake and theirs.

DARTERS

Who can resist the charm and beauty of those colorful little darlings, the darters (see two drawings right). They hang out in the riffles and sometimes make a nice meal for smallmouth bass or other predators that feed on what can be found there. There are several species of darters and sometimes it is hard to distinguish them. The ones below are likely an Orangethroat darter and a Variegate darter.

BUTTERFLIES AND DRAGONFLIES

So often we catch only a glimpse of these beautiful creatures that we hardly know them. What was that? Here are a few of the hundreds of insects that find the Little Miami River habitat to their liking.

Eastern Pondhawk

Eastern Amberwing

Spicebush Swallowtail

Zebra Swallowtail

HAWKS

When you think predator, you're usually thinking hawks. Besides the familiar Red-tailed Hawk, here are two that may be seen around the Little Miami River watershed, doing their best to keep rodents, fish, frogs and critters on their toes.

Sharp-shinned Hawk

Coopers Hawk

APPENDIX

REFERENCES AND RESOURCES

Journal of Spatial Hydrology, Bi-Annual publication of the American Spatial Hydrology Union, Inc - Warren County Local History by Dallas Bogan,

Warren County Historical Society - Riparian Forests and Benthic Macroinvertebrates in the Little Miami Scenic River Watershed By Bernie Daniel,

USEPA - Appendices to the Biological and Water Quality Study of the lower Little Miami River and Selected Tributaries 2007,

Ohio EPA - A Guide to Ohio Streams.

Ohio DNR - Biological and Water Quality Study of the Little Miami River – Peters Cartridge Area,

Ohio EPA - Biological Survey of the East Fork Little Miami River and O'Bannon Creek, Clermont County, Ohio, 2005,

Office of Environmental Quality - Seasonal Movements of Smallmouth Bass in Streams AFSS, 2002, by John Lyons and Paul Kanehl, Wisconsin DNR

The Haunted History of Glen Helen Nature Preserve in Yellow Springs, Ohio Glen Helen Ecology Institute, Glen Helen Throughout History -

Early Railways Of The Warren County Area by Dallas Bogan at rootsweb.ancestry.com

Smallmouth Bass Recruitment Variability and It's Relation to Stream Discharge in Three Virginia Rivers. Scott M. Smith -

Production Dynamics Of Smallmouth Bass In A Small Minnesota Stream Thomas F Waters, John P Kaehler, T. J. Palomis, Thomas J Kwak -

Occurrence and Distribution of Fish Species in the Great and Little Miami River Basins, Ohio and Indiana, Pre-1900 to 1998 By Stephanie Harrington

Distribution of the fishes of Indiana: Investigations of Indiana lakes and streams, Gerking, S.D., -

Helpful Websites on the LMR

REAL-TIME STREAMFLOW COMPARED TO HISTORICAL -

http://waterwatch.usgs.gov/?m=real&r=oh

FISHING REPORTS FROM ALL OVER OHIO -

http://www.ohiogamefishing.com/community/forumdisplay.php?f=10

CURRENT WATER LEVELS AND PREDICTIONS FOR OHIO STREAMS -

http://water.weather.gov/ahps2/index.php?wfo=iln

ECOLOGY AND HISTORY OF THE LMR BY STAN HEDEEN -

http://www.littlemiami.com/LITTLE%20MIAMI%20RIVER%20ECOLOGY%20AND%20HISTORY.pdf

WATERSHEDS OF OHIO -

http://www.digital-topo-maps.com/ Google map

PASTEL NATURAL HISTORY BLOG THAT OFTEN FEATURES THE LMR -

http://redandthepeanut.blogspot.com/search/label/Oil%20

GREAT BIRDING SITE -

http://cincinnatibirds.com

LOCAL FLY FISHING INFORMATION -

http://www.buckeyeflyfishers.com

LITTLE MIAMI TRAIL INFORMATION -

http://www.littlemiamistatepark.org

GUIDE TO OHIO FISH SPECIES -

http://www.dnr.state.oh.us/Home/species_a_to_z/AZFish/tabid/17913/Default.aspx

CONSERVATION EFFORTS ON THE LITTLE MIAMI -

http://www.littlemiami.org

The Little Miami Conservancy

Wild & Scenic River Conservation Since 1967

Join the Team !

Have you ever canoed or fished the Little Miami?
Have you ever biked the Little Miami Bike Trail?

If the answer is "YES!" to either question you will appreciate the efforts of the Little Miami Conservancy, a local nonprofit river conservation group who has been working diligently to restore and protect the Little Miami River, the region's only National Wild & Scenic River.

In 1967 the Little Miami Conservancy (LMC), formerly known as Little Miami Inc., was founded by river lovers who have translated their river passion into a permanent natural future for this national treasure. LMC's founder, newspaper editor Glenn Thompson, brought together many of his friends and colleagues to start the ball rolling 47 years ago and since then, this group of close to 500 supporters has accomplished wonders, natural wonders, along this exceptional river.

The Little Miami Conservancy's Magrish Preserve was transferred to the City of Cincinnati near Lunken Airport for permanent preservation in 1991.

After leading the charge to achieve National Wild & Scenic River designation (the first in Ohio) in 1973, LMC headed up the effort to create the Little Miami State Park Trail in 1983. Sending a team to Washington, DC and Columbus, Ohio $2 million was earmarked and forwarded to the Ohio Department of Natural Resources (ODNR) to purchase over 40 miles of abandoned Penn Central rail line along the Little Miami. This was the first "Rails to Trails" project in Ohio!

LMC Executive Director Eric B. Partee and the

Little Miami Conservancy Tucker Preserve in Warren County

LMC Board of Directors have been raising funds (both private and public) to acquire riverfront lands, plant trees, prairies, wildflowers and save wetlands and more along the 105-mile-long river corridor flowing through five counties in Southwest Ohio.

The Little Miami Conservancy has acquired over 100 nature preserves along the Little Miami and, in partnership with local park districts and ODNR, over 53% of the riverfront forest lands along the river's 105 mile length are now permanently preserved!

Little Miami Conservancy volunteers plant future forests

"There's no better single way to save a river than to preserve the trees which line that river", according to Eric B. Partee, LMC Executive Director since 1982.

In 2011 LMC planted over 40,000 trees along the Little Miami and planted 200 acres of native prairie grasses. These lands are critical habitat to 255 bird species that live and migrate through the Little Miami corridor. Great Blue Herons, hawks, warblers, woodpeckers, and more recently the Bald Eagle, call the Little Miami "home" for all or part of the year.

One of LMC's newest nature preserves, the 82-acre Tecumseh Preserve, is located at Oldtown north of Xenia, Ohio at the site of the old Shawnee capital

land at the preserve. LMC member support allows the organization to manage this restored habitat to benefit wildlife and the river.

On October 5, 2013 LMC was joined by the Eastern Shawnee Tribe from Oklahoma, public officials and 150 supporters to dedicate the preserve in honor of Tecumseh and the river. Eastern Shawnee National Chief Enyart stated, "You honor us by your conservation efforts here."

LMC also partnered with Warren County officials to acquire a small 1.4 acre property upstream from Morrow. The land is bordered on one side by the river and by the bike trail on the other.

"It was a mess", Partee proclaimed, "The biggest eyesore along the Little Miami." The largest building was about to fall into the river. LMC got to work moving out several semi-trailers, an old school bus, an RV, seven huge "dragon box" dumpsters of trash and razed 4 buildings.

Over 40 volunteers helped clear the property of items ranging from plastic barrels to glass bottles which was a tremendous help.

"The project wasn't cheap", Partee notes, "It cost LMC $20,000, all paid for by LMC members. Our

Little Miami Conservancy Beckley Preserve in Clark County

site where the Shawnee leader Tecumseh was born. Typical of LMC's approach, this preserve was the result of a partnership with local, state and other local conservation organizations to fund the purchase and restoration of this spectacular riverfront area. LMC planted 10,000 trees (mostly oaks) and 45 acres of native warm-season prairie grasses and wildflowers to compliment an existing 17 acre wet-

members have contributed financially to numerous similar restoration projects over the years leading to the removal of many abandoned buildings and restoring the natural beauty that the river enjoyed over 200 years ago."

Ohio EPA has found the endangered Blue Sucker in the Lower Little Miami National Wild & Scenic River in Cincinnati

Ohio's Largest Exceptional Warm Water Habitat
A mere 10% of Ohio's streams are labeled "exceptional warm water habitat" making up the best of Ohio's stream ecosystems. The Little Miami is the longest stretch of river in this distinguished category. Some 83 fish species, and 36 species of fresh water mussels live below the surface of the Little Miami along with hundreds of additional species of aquatic insects. It is the health of these species that guides the efforts of Ohio EPA and LMC to restore and keep the river in full ecological health.

Back in 1983 only 3% of the Little Miami's length met Ohio EPA chemical and biological standards. Studies showed that phosphorus was the principal contaminant degrading the river. This nutrient would enter the river and promote algae growth which would take dissolved oxygen levels to near zero parts per million on several river segments during periods of summer low flow. A comprehensive strategy was needed.

In the succeeding years Ohio EPA and LMC met with public officials to discuss the needed restoration work. LMC agreed to continue its habitat protection and restoration projects. NRCS and County Soil and Water Conservation Districts agreed to continue their work with local farmers to implement farm conservation plans. Local officials agreed to ratchet down the amounts of phosphorus coming out of waste water treatment plants.

As a result of this partnership the river responded. In 2007 Ohio EPA sampling and analysis concluded that 97% of the Little Miami's length was in "full attainment" of the agency's chemical and biological standards!

LMC continues to work with public officials and others to assure that this renewed ecosystem remains healthy as the Little Miami watershed continues to see development spread easterly from the Cincinnati and Dayton metropolitan areas.

You CAN help...
Join the Team!

Please join LMC at **www.littlemiami.org** where you will learn about volunteer opportunities, obtain the latest river news, download quality river maps, and donate to become an LMC member.

LMC memberships start at $25, although many donate $100 or more annually. Every "drop in the bucket" makes a difference for this national treasure.

You can leave your legacy along the Little Miami, naturally! Please join the Little Miami Conservancy!

Little Miami Conservancy members on one of many annual floats

Little Miami Wild & Scenic River

Upper River - Clifton to Spring Valley - Greene County

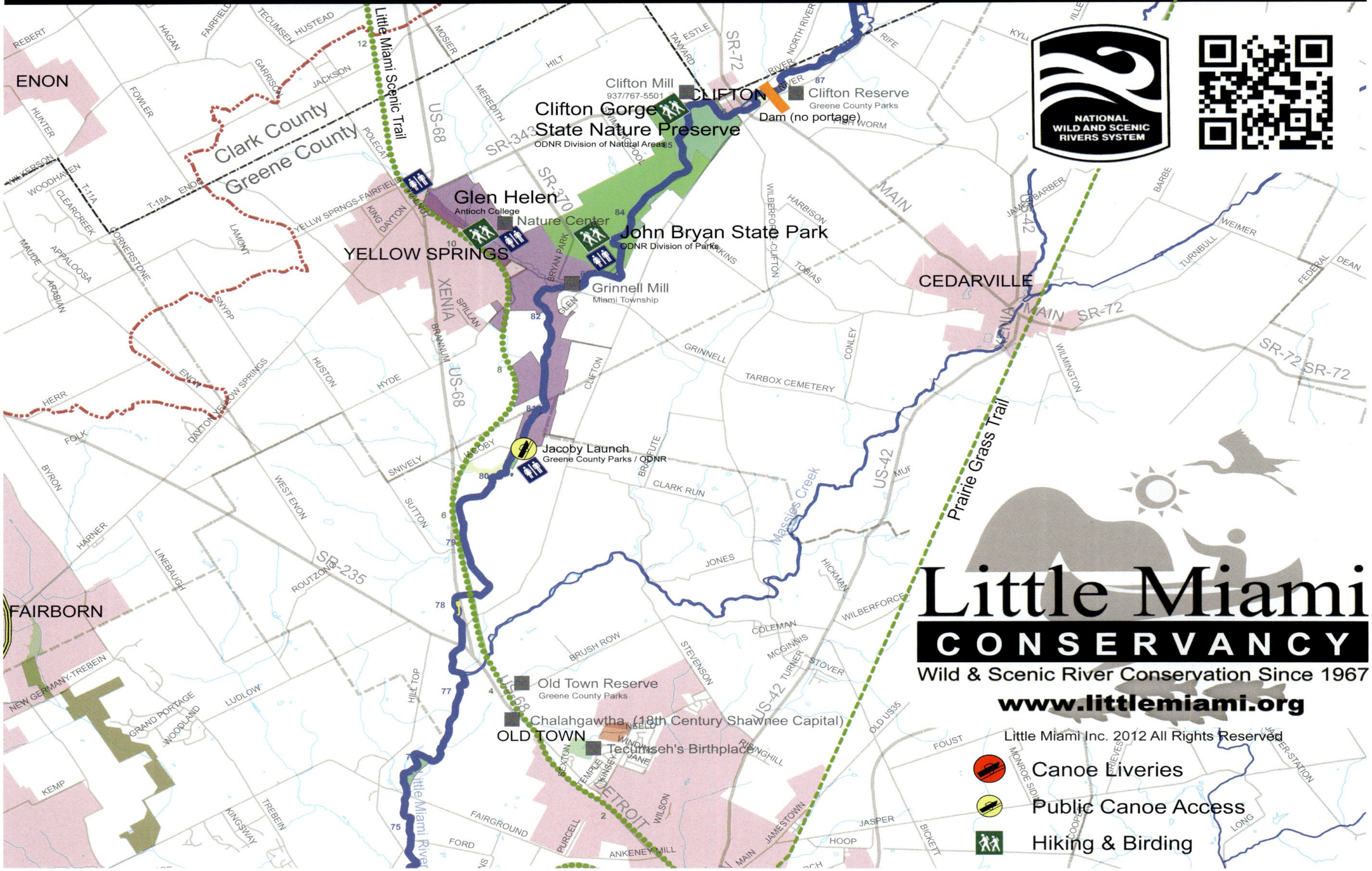

National Wild and Scenic Rivers System

Little Miami CONSERVANCY

Wild & Scenic River Conservation Since 1967

www.littlemiami.org

Canoe Liveries

Public Canoe Access

Hiking & Birding

Prairie Grass Trail

CEDARVILLE

SR-72

US-42

XENIA

WILMINGTON

Clifton Reserve
Greene County Parks

Dam (no portage)

Clifton Mill
937/767-5501

Clifton Gorge
State Nature Preserve
ODNR Division of Natural Areas

John Bryan State Park
ODNR Division of Parks

Grinnell Mill
Miami Township

Glen Helen
Nature Center
Antioch College

YELLOW SPRINGS

Jacoby Launch
Greene County Parks / ODNR

Old Town Reserve
Greene County Parks

Chalahgawtha (18th Century Shawnee Capital)
Tecumseh's Birthplace

OLD TOWN

US-68

XENIA

DETROIT

FAIRBORN

ENON

Clark County

Greene County

Little Miami Scenic Trail

Little Miami River

US-68

SR-235

SR-370

SR-343

SR-72

US-42

100

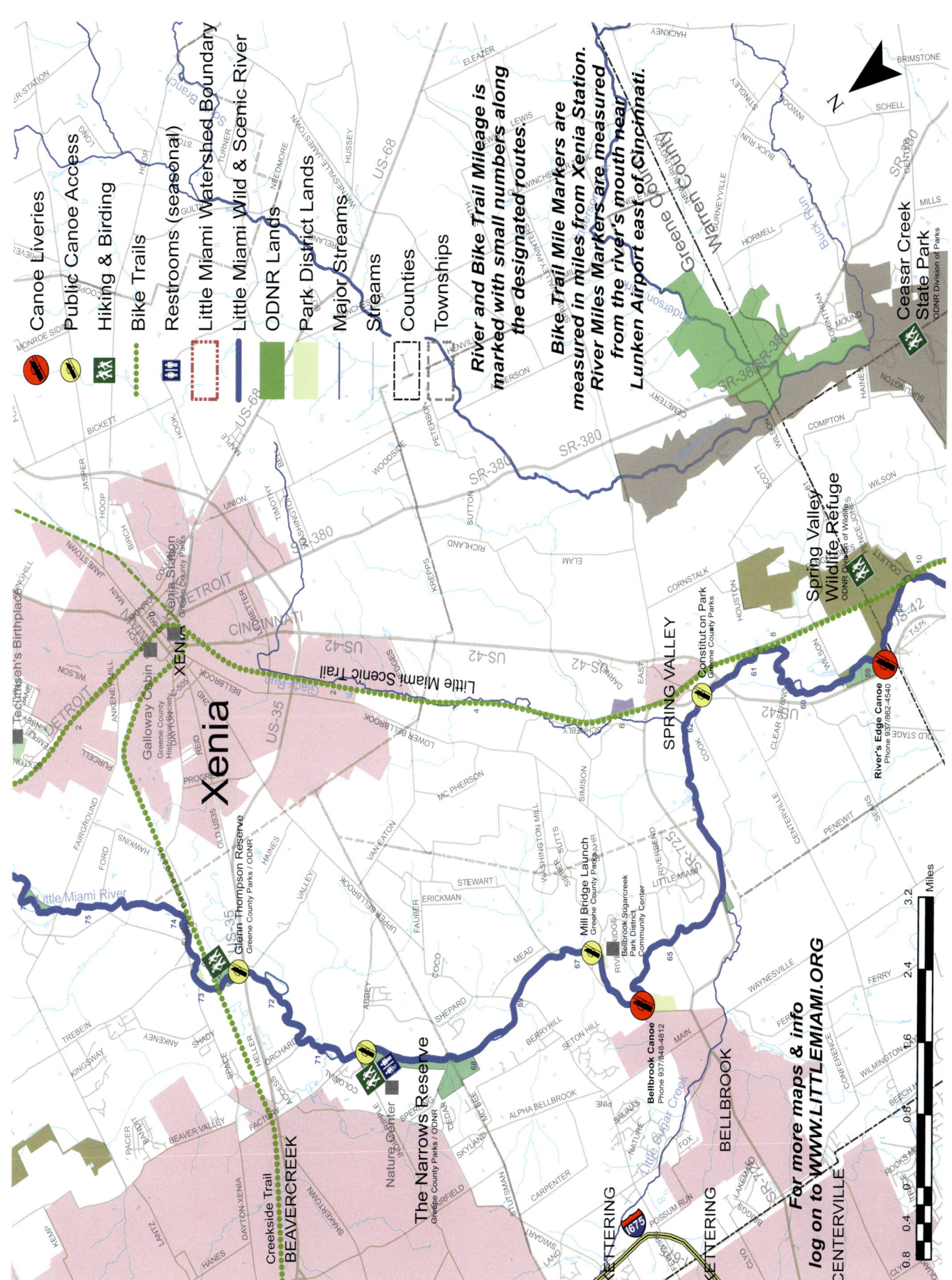

Legend:

- Canoe Liveries
- Public Canoe Access
- Hiking & Birding
- Bike Trails
- Restrooms (seasonal)
- Little Miami Watershed Boundary
- Little Miami Wild & Scenic River
- ODNR Lands
- Park District Lands
- Major Streams
- Streams
- Counties
- Townships

River and Bike Trail Mileage is marked with small numbers along the designated routes.

Bike Trail Mile Markers are measured in miles from Xenia Station. River Miles Markers are measured from the river's mouth near Lunken Airport east of Cincinnati.

Ceasar Creek State Park
ODNR Division of Parks

Spring Valley Wildlife Refuge
ODNR Division of Wildlife

River's Edge Canoe
Phone 937/862-4540

Constitution Park
Greene County Parks

SPRING VALLEY

XENIA

Xenia Station
Greene County Parks

Galloway Cabin
Greene County
Historical Society

Tecumseh's Birthplace

DETROIT

CINCINNATI

Little Miami Scenic Trail

Little Miami River

Glenn Thompson Reserve
Greene County Parks / ODNR

Mill Bridge Launch
Greene County Parks

Bellbrook Sugarcreek
Park District
Community Center

The Narrows Reserve
Greene County Parks / ODNR

Nature Center

Creekside Trail

BEAVERCREEK

Bellbrook Canoe
Phone 937/848-4812

BELLBROOK

Little Sugar Creek

KETTERING

CENTERVILLE

For more maps & info log on to WWW.LITTLEMIAMI.ORG

Miles
0.4 0.8 1.6 2.4 3.2

101

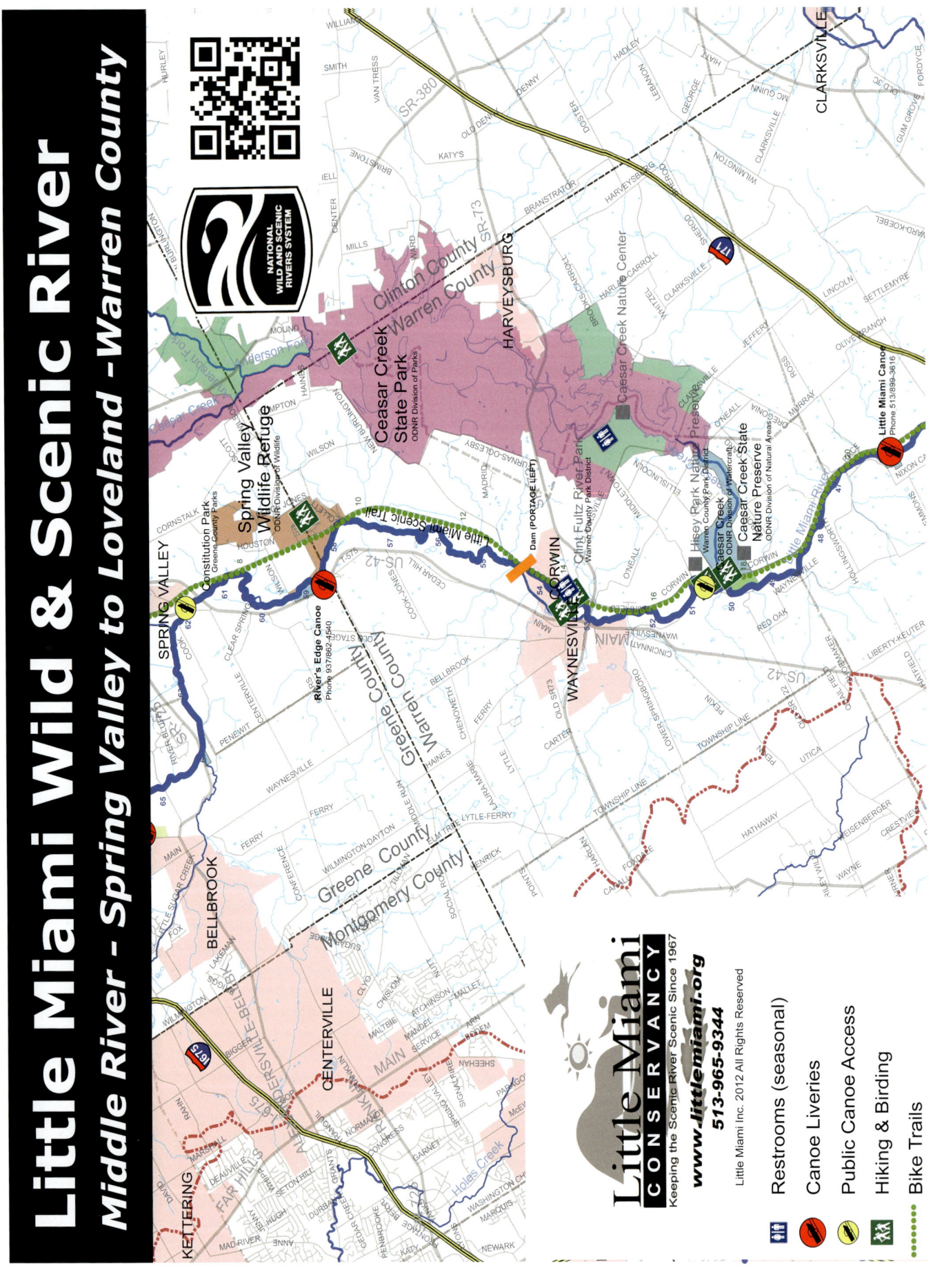

Little Miami Wild & Scenic River

Middle River – Spring Valley to Loveland -Warren County

NATIONAL WILD AND SCENIC RIVERS SYSTEM

Little Miami
CONSERVANCY

Keeping the Scenic River Scenic Since 1967

www.littlemiami.org

513-965-9344

Little Miami Inc. 2012 All Rights Reserved

- Restrooms (seasonal)
- Canoe Liveries
- Public Canoe Access
- Hiking & Birding
- Bike Trails

River's Edge Canoe
Phone 937/862-4540

Little Miami Canoe
Phone 513/899-3616

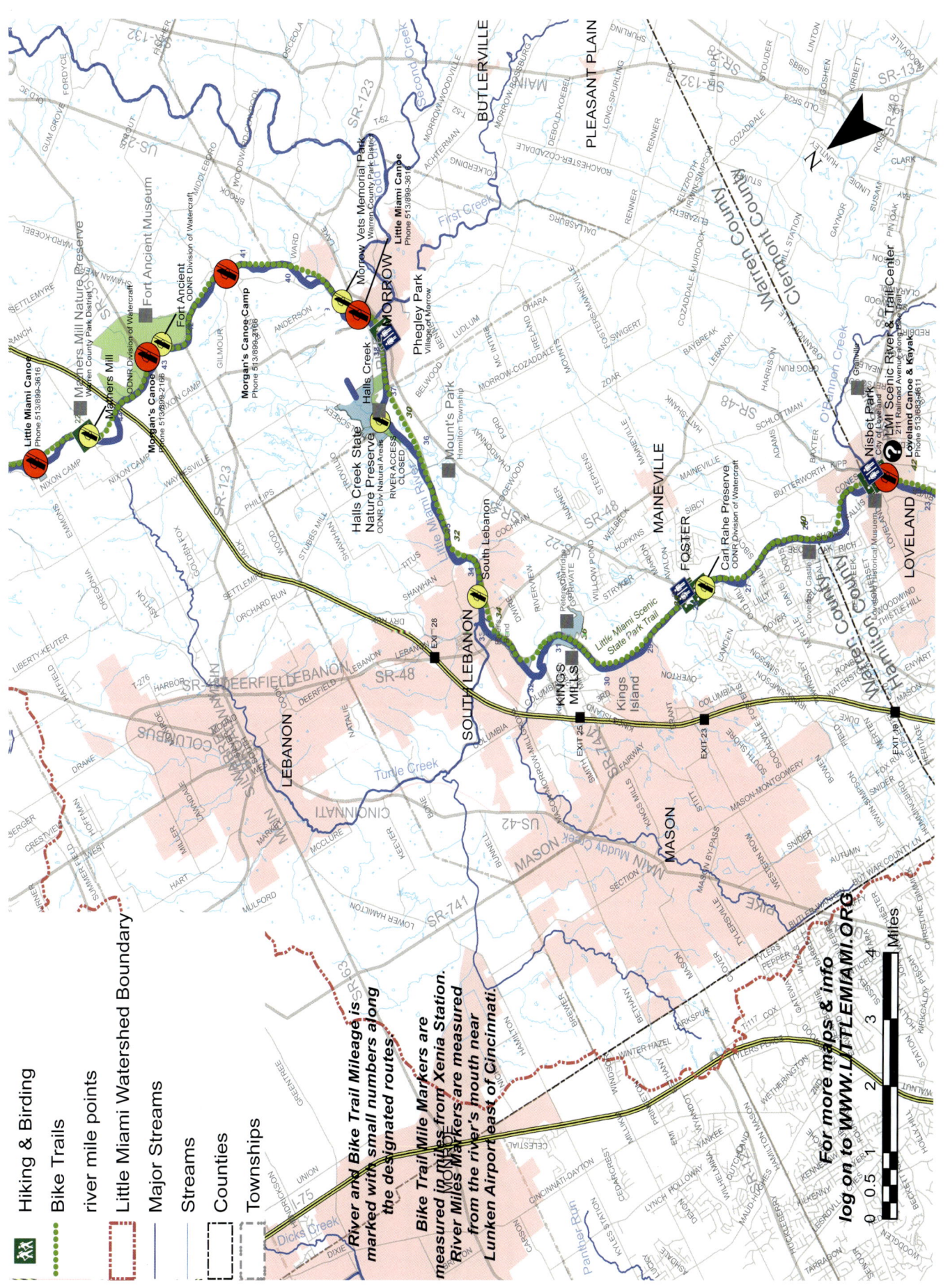

Legend

Hiking & Birding

Bike Trails ●●●●●

river mile points

Little Miami Watershed Boundary ▭▭

Major Streams ▬▬

Streams ▬▬

Counties ▭▭

Townships ▭▭

River and Bike Trail Mileage is marked with small numbers along the designated routes.

Bike Trail Mile Markers are measured in miles from Xenia Station. River Mile Markers are measured from the river's mouth near Lunken Airport east of Cincinnati.

For more maps & info log on to WWW.LITTLEMIAMI.ORG

Miles
0 0.5 1 2 3 4

Little Miami Wild & Scenic River

Lower Little Miami – Morrow downstream to Cincinnati

Trail Mileage Chart

Little Miami Scenic Trail
(miles from Loveland)

Urbana via Simon Kenton Trail	81.7
Buck Creek State Park	69.1
via Buck Creek Trail	
Springfield (downtown)	63.1
Beatty	59.3
Yellow Springs	53.7
Xenia Station	43.9
Spring Valley	37.2
Corwin	27.6
Morrow	13.7
Loveland	0.0
Milford	8.5
Newtown	13.1

Ohio to Erie Trail
(miles from Xenia Station)

Cedarville	7.8
South Charleston	18.4
London	28.7

Creekside Trail
(connector trail from the Little Miami Trail at Xenia Station west to Dayton;

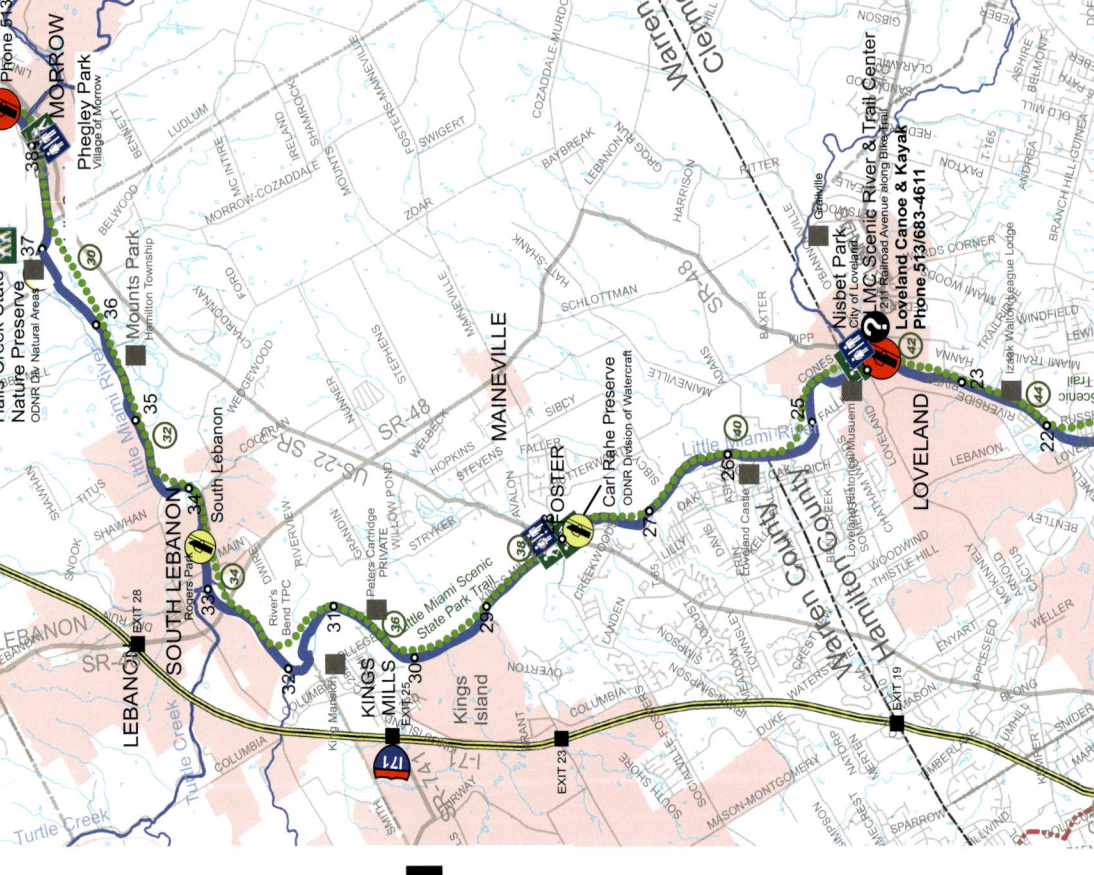

Little Miami Canoe
Phone 513/899-3616

Halls Creek State Nature Preserve
ODNR Div Natural Areas

Phegley Park
Village of Morrow

Mounts Park
Hamilton Township

South Lebanon

Rogers Park

Peters Cartridge
PRIVATE

Little Miami Scenic
State Park Trail

Carl Rahe Preserve
ODNR Division of Watercraft

Nisbet Park
City of Loveland

Loveland Historical Museum

LMC Scenic River & Trail Center
231 Railroad Avenue along Bike Trail

Loveland Canoe & Kayak
Phone 513/683-4611

 Canoe Liveries

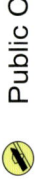 Public Canoe Access

Hiking & Birding

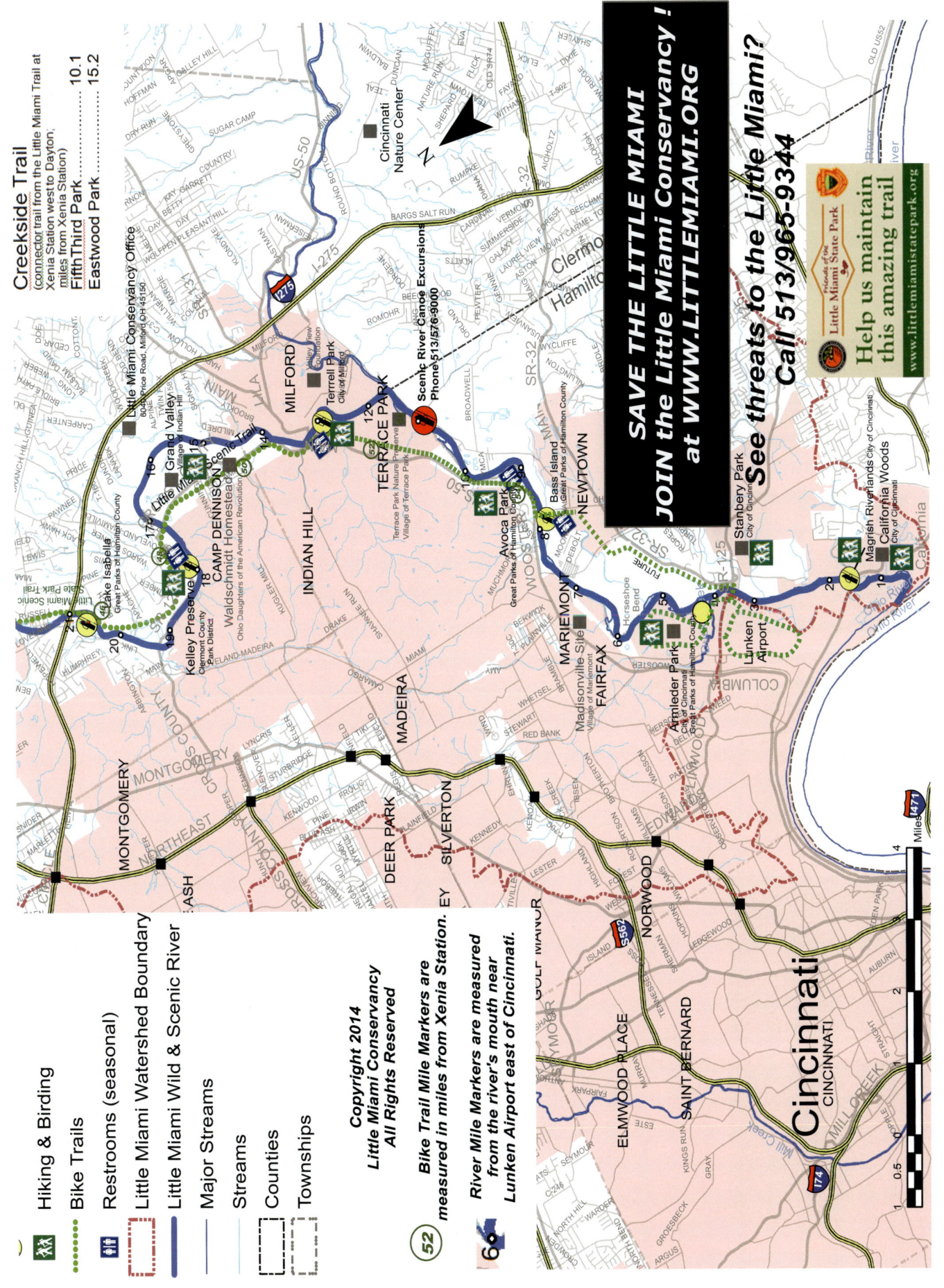

Creekside Trail

(connector trail from the Little Miami Trail at
Xenia Station west to Dayton;
miles from Xenia Station)

Fifth Third Park 10.1
Eastwood Park 15.2

SAVE THE LITTLE MIAMI
JOIN the Little Miami Conservancy !
at WWW.LITTLEMIAMI.ORG

See threats to the Little Miami?
Call 513/965-9344

Help us maintain
this amazing trail
www.littlemiamistatepark.org

Legend:

- Hiking & Birding
- Bike Trails
- Restrooms (seasonal)
- Little Miami Watershed Boundary
- Little Miami Wild & Scenic River
- Major Streams
- Streams
- Counties
- Townships

Copyright 2014
Little Miami Conservancy
All Rights Reserved

52 Bike Trail Mile Markers are
measured in miles from Xenia Station.

6 River Mile Markers are
measured from the river's mouth near
Lunken Airport east of Cincinnati.

Canoe Rentals on the Little Miami

(Upstream to Downstream)

Each canoe rental generally offers canoes, kayaks and multi-person rafts along with overnight camping.
Exact locations of each rental can be found on the maps on Pages 100 - 105

	Name	Phone, Web URL, County
	**Bellbrook Canoe Rental**	937-848-4812 www.bellbrookcanoerental.com Greene
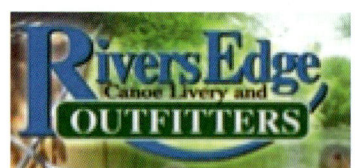	**RiversEdge Canoe Livery & Outfitters**	937-903-6468 www.riversedgeoutfitters.com Greene, Warren
	**Little Miami River Canoe Rental**	513-899-3616 www.littlemiamicanoe.com Warren
	**Morgan's Outdoor Adventures**	513-932-7658 www.morganscanoe.com Warren
	**Loveland Canoe & Kayak**	513-683-4611 www.lovelandcanoe.com Warren, Clermont, Hamilton
	**Scenic River Canoe Excursions**	513-576-9000 www.scenicrivercanoe.com Hamilton, Clermont

Supporters & Sponsors

The author and the Little Miami Conservancy gratefully acknowledge
support and encouragement from the following ad sponsors for this
book and for LMC restoration and protection efforts on the
Little Miami National Wild & Scenic River since 1967.

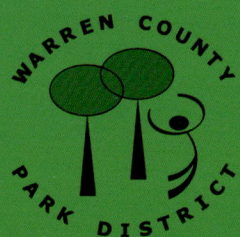

Working together by providing the finest Parks, Programs, and Recreational Facilities for our community of Warren County.

Larry Easterly
Park District
Director

Fred Bay
County Park
Commissioner

Jeff Blazey
County Park
Commissioner

Ben Yoder
County Park
Commissioner

Pat South
County
Commissioner

Tom Ariss
County
Commissioner

Dave Young
County
Commissioner

The National and Scenic Little Miami River

The **Warren County Board of Commissioners** and the **Warren County Park District** are proud to call this majestic river part of our home.

Bowman Park
200 Corwin Ave, Waynesville, Ohio

Mathers Mill Nature Preserve
5349 Wilmington Rd, Oregonia, Ohio

Clint Fultz River Park
6102 Corwin Ave, Corwin, Ohio

Morrow Veteran's Park
200 Hamlin St and 104 Lincoln St, Morrow, Ohio

Photos are courtesy of Bob Young (local river enthusiast).